AVIATE

NAVIGATE

COMMUNICATE

AVIATE
NAVIGATE
COMMUNICATE

An unlikely Journey from a Piper Cub pilot to B-747 Captain. A lot things had to go right including good health and vision and the proper age.

A Memoir

by

Jerry Lawler
Captain TWA retired

DEDICATION

To my wife, Sue George Lawler, who made this journey possible She was my first passenger as a Private Pilot and she was a passenger on my last flight as a TWA pilot. She allowed me to follow my dream while she taught school and managed our family.

CONTENTS

CHAPTER 1

PRE-FLIGHT

Can flying be in your blood? Why was I fascinated with airplanes? Maybe it was watching newsreel films of bombs dropping through the air and then exploding on Germany at the end of World War II. Movies taken from the cockpit of fighter planes shooting up moving railroad trains fascinated me. My family grew up in Chicago under the flight path of Midway Airport, then the world's busiest. In grade school I was a passenger on a flight from Chicago's Midway Airport to Florida. I could not get enough of looking out the window. When I did close my eyes, I could feel the gentle air turbulence and the engine vibrations.

A neighbor took me for a ride in a rented Piper Cub. We flew with the side door open and I was sorely disappointed when we landed. In high school I started getting catalogs from flying schools. Propeller driven Constellations and DC-6s would fly right over our house on approach to Midway airport. I told a classmate of mine that I would fly those someday. One of my favorite things to do was to go to 63rd and Cicero and watch the planes takeoff and land at Midway airport.

My father was a medical doctor and he expected me to follow in his path. I was in my second year of Pre-Med at Loyola University in Chicago when my father suddenly passed away at 58 years of age. At that time, a student could be accepted into Loyola Dental School with good grades after 2 years of under-graduate school. Since I did not have the burning desire for a medical career, I decided to go to dental school. I also decided to learn how to fly.

Within a few months I visited Howell Airport to inquire about flying lessons. Willie Howell, the owner, put me in a Piper Cub with an instructor before I could ask any questions. With less than 8 hours of instruction, and 13 days later, I flew the airplane by myself. Your first "solo" flight is a memorable event. I flew around the airport and made a total of three take offs landings by myself. I felt a great sense of accomplishment and also confident that it was something that I could do. So I had earned my Student Pilot Certificate. My mother knew nothing of my flying lessons. It wasn't until I ran up a large bill

at the airport that I asked my mother for financial help. In her naturally kind way, she agreed. I was able to pay her back many times over the years with free travel that she enjoyed flying around the world sitting in First Class on a TWA jet.

In 1959, I earned my Private Pilot Certificate which allows you to carry passengers. Willie Howell administered the flight check, and that same day, I took a beautiful girl named Sue George up as my first passenger. At that time, jet airliners were replacing propeller driven airliners. Jets could fly twice as fast and carry twice as many passengers and therefore less pilots were needed.

I spent a year at dental school where I did well scholastically, but I felt that I did not have the hands to be a good dentist. I am not mechanically inclined, nor do I possess the patience necessary to fix things with my hands. The dental profession was fortunate that I withdrew after I completed one year. One thing I did do during that year was to continue flying. Many times I would cut the anatomy lab where we worked on cadavers to go flying.

Sue George graduated from Mount Mary College with a degree in teaching. My degree was a Bachelor of Science degree with a major in Biology. Sue and I were married in 1963. Sue was teaching 4th grade and I was working for Loyola University wishing for a job in aviation.

In November of 1963. I was reading the Chicago Tribune Want Ads under Aviation. There was a two line ad that TWA would be hiring flight deck crewmembers. They had not hired any pilots in the last 6 years. I stopped at the TWA ticket office in downtown Chicago and picked up an application for employment. The pilot application required a Commercial pilot certificate with an Instrument Rating. I did not have these but I knew where I could train for them. The problem was the cost.

Sue had saved $3,000.00 from teaching. That was all the money we had. I sat on the floor of our third floor apartment, looked up at Sue sitting on the couch and asked her if I could use the money to get the licenses that I needed to apply to TWA. There was absolutely no guarantee the I would get hired even if I obtained the training. However, I would commit to finding a job in aviation. Sue knew of my desire to be an airline pilot. She was the first passenger I took up after I received my Private pilot license. To my amazement, she agreed. There were no conditions, no making me feel like I owed her big time. Follow your dream.

Fortunately there was a well regarded instrument training school located at Midway Airport. Aviation Training Enterprises, known as ATE, offered a guaranteed Instrument rating for about $1,000.00. The flat price included unlimited groundschool and simulator time. I wanted to get all I could get, so I signed up for the guaranteed course. I did not want the pressure of paying for each hour of training.

In order to safely fly in clouds and bad weather, a pilot must possess an Instrument rating. You fly by looking at the airplane instruments when you cannot see outside. There are lots of instruments and you must develop what is called a scan pattern. First you learn how to keep the wings level by using an artificial horizon or

3

what today is called an Attitude Indicator. The top half of the instrument is blue to represent the sky, while the bottom half is brown to represent the ground.

The wings are depicted in orange with a dot in the center to represent the nose of the aircraft. The position of the nose in relation to the horizon is called pitch. The position of the wings in relation to the horizon is called roll.

Located on one side of the attitude indicator is the altimeter which give the height of the airplane over the earth. On the other side is the airspeed indicator which indicates how fast the airplane is flying. Right below the attitude indicator is the compass which gives the direction the airplane is flying. So you have three instruments on the top and one below. That is the shape of a "T." So we use what we call a "T" pattern scan. There are other instruments on each side of the compass. These are secondary instruments in the scan.

The attitude indicator is the main instrument to look at. If the wings are level, the airplane is going straight ahead and not turning. Therefore the compass will not move. If the nose dot is on the horizon, the aircraft is not climbing or descending, therefore the altimeter will not change. The airspeed will not change if the nose is on the horizon and the throttle is not moved.

So the "T" scan is simple. Start with the attitude indicator then check the altimeter and right back to the attitude indicator. Check the airspeed indicator and right back to the attitude indicator. Check the compass and right back to the attitude indicator. Sounds simple and it really works.

Then you learn to fly a course by using a compass. You fly one of the 360 degrees of the compass.. You have to learn to climb and descend using a vertical speed indicator. You also have to monitor engine instruments. You also have to talk on the radio with Air Traffic Control. You develop three priorities: Aviate, Navigate, Communicate. In other words, fly the airplane first. Don't get fixated on one instrument and forget what the airplane is doing. The next priority is to know where

you are going i.e.Navigate. Finally, and least important, is to Communicate with Air Traffic Control. Aviate, Navigate, Communicate.

Never before did I dive into a program with such enthusiasm. Ground school subjects included weather, navigation, regulations, aircraft systems, etc. In the simulator you learned to fly straight and level, turns to specific headings, descents to altitude, holding procedures, and instrument approaches to the airport. Once you are proficient in the simulator, you now do the same in an airplane. I was an avid student and I earned my Instrument Rating on February 10, 1964.

Still I had to pay for more training. In order to receive compensation for flying an airplane, you need a Commercial Pilot Certificate. One year and one day after Sue and I were married, I earned my Commercial Pilot Certificate on February 24, 1964. Now I could apply to TWA. Here's hoping I get hired since I spent most of our money. Thank God Sue is teaching.

CHAPTER 2

TWA FLIGHT ENGINEER

The application was sent to TWA. Surprisingly, shortly afterward, a letter arrived from TWA inviting me for an interview on April 2, 1964. Twenty applicants arrived for the process held in a hanger at the Kansas City airport. There was a written test followed by some interviews with some human resources personnel. They check your log books and see if you really have the proper certificates. If you got past HR, you got to meet the chief pilot. I thought he would ask me about my flying but he was more interested in my education. He also wanted to know if my wife was comfortable with my flying. At the end of the day, the twenty applicants re-assembled in a class room. Two of us were called out of the room by the HR person. I assumed that we were being eliminated. However, the HR guy congratulated us and said the other applicants were being sent home. The other pilot that would go on to phase two with me was an Air Force B-47 pilot. Wow, a single engine propeller pilot and a 6 engine jet pilot.

The HR guy told me that the chief pilot liked my attitude. Also, TWA insisted on a college degree for civilian trained pilots like myself. Graduating from a university showed commitment and commitment would be needed to complete TWA's rigorous training program. So the next day I took a very extensive physical and then returned home anxious to know if I would make it or not.

By now I had left Loyola and was very concerned about my future. Thank God Sue had a good job. We lived in a three story apartment building with many mail boxes in the small lobby. There was always lots of junk mail laying around. I noticed a letter jammed under some junk mail that had a red TWA border on it. My heart jumped when I saw my name on it. I tore it open. TWA congratulated me on being accepted and told me to report to Kansas City on June 15th. The class would find out the first day what airplane and what position we would be trained to fly. Immediately I drove out to Sue's school, told the principal that I had to see her for one minute.After running to her classroom, I told her that I got hired. A very happy moment in my life.

School was out and Sue and I drove down to Kansas City in our white Chevy convertible. It is hot in Kansas City in the summer. We rented an apartment in a very up-scale building close to the TWA Training Center. Two Kansas City professional baseball players lived there. This building was on a hill that overlooked the airport. It also had a beautiful pool.

At the time that I got hired with TWA, there was a bitter battle going on in the airline cockpits between the pilots and the flight engineers. They each had their own union. With the 4-engine jets coming on line, the pilots union wanted the flight engineers be pilot qualified. The pilot union did this to protect pilot jobs in case there was a reduction of flying. The pilots could move back to the flight engineer position. The flight engineers wanted licensed mechanics in the position. It was a conflict that ended when President Kennedy sided with the pilots. JFK signed a law that there had to be three qualified pilots in each 4-engine jet airliner.

Most of TWA's flight engineers were not qualified pilots. So on jet flights where the flight engineer was not a qualified pilot, a fourth crewmember was required to ride in the observer's seat. This crewmember was called a second officer. TWA was taking delivery of many new jets and they needed more flight crewmembers. We were called "new-hires." The first few "new-hire" classes were trained to be flight engineers on the Lockheed Constellation, a four-engine propeller airplane with the distinctive three tails. Then they hired several classes of second officers for the Boeing 707 and Convair 880.

7

The TWA Training Center was an eight story building located in downtown Kansas City, Missouri. It contained many classrooms with training devices, cabin mock-ups for evacuation training, and aircraft simulators. The pilots used the first six floors and the

Hostesses (that is what they were called in those days) trained on the top two floors. TWA did not try to save money in training their crewmembers because they recognized the importance of well trained crewmembers. The following sign greeted us every day that we entered the building: "Persistent training is the key to TWA excellence and the foundation of public trust in all of us."

The June 15th class was assigned to be Lockheed Constellation flight engineers. The previous 7 classes were trained as Second Officers. Rats, the Second Officer class before me got to ride around in new jets while I was going to be a flight engineer on a dated propeller plane. It really didn't matter, I was thrilled to be hired in any position.

There were 20 new hires in my class with an incredible mix. There were five Air Force pilots, five Navy pilots, five Marine pilots, and five civilian pilots. Our all important seniority number on the pilot roster is based on your age in your new hire class. The civilian pilots were the youngest and I was the second oldest of the five. So I was pretty far down the list in my class. Once again, I didn't care, I couldn't believe I was going to be an airline pilot.

The training course was set up to be a four month program. The airlines do not make any money from your services while you are in training. Therefore, the training is designed to give you the maximum amount of information in the minimum amount of time. Now I realized why TWA insisted on having a college degree. We were told that the training we would accomplish in four months would require two years at the University of Michigan. TWA was making an investment in us, and once hired, they did not want us to withdraw. Again, they wanted young pilots so they would have many years of return on their investment.

It was not long before I realized that I might be in over my head. The military guys all came in with extensive training from the military. Two of the civilian pilots had already worked as pilots for other airlines. Another civilian pilot had just graduated from the University of Illinois with a degree in mechanical engineering. His father owned an airport and he had much more flying time than I did. He would be a great help to me in the upcoming training. Once again, this Flight Engineer course was not designed for pilots, it was designed for people with FAA mechanic licenses. I had zero mechanical background.

There was a reason that I never worked with tools. As a doctor, my father had some patients who could not always afford to pay for his services. So, many times he was paid by having chores done around our house by his patients. I did not know the names of many tools. It was a joke in my new-hire class that I did not know what a Phillips screwdriver was.

The first six weeks consisted of ground school, as opposed to in-flight training which would come later. We had to learn every system of the Constellation. We had the electrical system which controlled lighting and powered instruments, the hydraulic systems that operated flight controls and raised and lowered the landing gear wheels, the fuel and oil systems to power the engines, the pneumatic system that pressurized the airplane, the air-conditioning system that heated and cooled the airplane, the electronics system that operated the aircraft radios, the anti-ice system that heated probes and kept ice off of the wings and propellers, and others referred to as small systems. We had to learn all about government regulations that applied to the airlines, and believe me, there are lots of regulations. We had to pass a test on Morris Code, which I have long forgotten. We also had to learn the company policies and procedures. There is one thing to keep in mind about training at TWA, you either made it or you were dismissed. But it was ok to fail a written or oral test along the way. Most everyone did.

After completing ground school, we had to pass the FAA Flight Engineer written test. This was another challenge that those hired as Second Officers did not have to endure. This is a government test that had little resemblance to the real world. It came in 10 parts and I was given the opportunity to take 3 of the parts over again. At least I was not alone. Several of my classmates joined me in retaking parts of the written exam. I passed them on the retake, but it made me nervous. Again, this test was designed for mechanics, not pilots.

With all the ground testing competed, we entered the simulator phase of our training. The simulator is an exact duplicate of the cockpit of the Constellation. It simulates flight and all the instruments act just as they would in a real airplane. Now we put into practice what we learned in ground school. Only now it is totally different because things are really happening and you have to deal with them. The first thing the flight engineer does is conduct a "walk around" and examine the exterior of the airplane. You look for obvious fluid leaks from the airplane. Hydraulic fluid is highly toxic and you do not want to have it drop on you. You also look for oil leaks. You check the tires and the multiple openings on the airplane and you have to know the purpose for each opening. You will come back later to check the fuel tanks. Since this was a simulator, some of these chores would have to be done on a real airplane.

There were many things to check in the cockpit, so to make sure we did not miss anything, we would use a "flow pattern." Learning flow patterns became very important and they were used every time you operated an airplane. If you know what the cockpit of an airliner looks like, you know that there are multiple gauges and dials to look at. All the lights are checked to see if they are working. A warning light does not do much good if it is burned out and fails to send a warning. Many years ago an Eastern Airlines L-1011 crashed in the Everglades because the green landing gear down safe light was burned out and the flight crew got distracted as they all looked at the problem. Remember the first rule is to Aviate-fly the airplane. Back to the flow pattern. The flight engineer checks the oxygen system. There is a system for the passengers and there is a different type of system for the cockpit crew. The oxygen for the passengers is used in case of a rapid decompression. The flight crew oxygen is used for the same purpose but it can also be used if there is smoke in the cockpit. The pilots check their own masks so that germs are not spread around. The engineer also checks the passenger cabin.

The pilots do their flow patterns and the engineer checks his instruments with a flow pattern. At some point, the captain will call for the "Before Starting Engines Checklist."This checklist is read aloud by the flight engineer. What we are checking is to see if the item is completed. It is not something you do as the checklist is read. It is basically a challenge and response method. The engineer will say "Gear lever and lights." The captain will respond "Down and checked." The first check list covers about 30 items. When the pilot and engineer checklist are completed, it is time to start the engines.

The engineer is mostly responsible for starting the engines on the Constellation. On the jet airplanes, it is up to the pilots. The engineer has to be in contact by an interphone with a maintenance person on the ground standing by the engine. A spinning propeller is deadly and we have to make sure the area is clear before we rotate the propeller. When the person on the ground says it is clear, the engineer moves a switch that starts the propeller moving. The ground person watches the engine rotate and after 8 revolutions he calls out "eight blades." This is the signal for the engineer to move another switch that will introduce fuel and ignition to the engine. Hopefully, after a lot of belching and smoking, the engine will start. We are all on the lookout for a hot start or a fire in the engine. We practice for fires in the simulator.

After the engine is started, the engineer runs another flow pattern checking the oil pressure, the electrical supply, and other things like the cylinder head temperatures. Once that engine looks ok, you start the other three in the same way. After they are all started, the captain calls for the "After starting engines checklist." Once again it is a challenge and response to see that everything has already been accomplished.

Now it is time to taxi to the departure runway. The airplane is configured to fly by extending wing flaps that will give added lift during take off. Once again, flow patterns are followed by the pilots and engineer. The "Taxi checklist" is read and responded to indicate the item has been accomplished.

Jet airplanes can take off as soon as they reach the runway. This is not true on propeller airplanes. The Constellation had to pull into an area adjacent to the runway end called the "run-up block." This is where the engines are run-up to a set power to check to see if all the systems were operating properly. When that was accomplished and given permission to take off, the "Before takeoff checklist" was read.

According to safety experts, there are 11 crucial minutes of a flight when you need to be especially alert on an airplane. The 3 minutes during takeoff and the final 8 minutes before landing are when 80% of airplane accidents occur. We refer to that as "plus 3 minus 8." During takeoff the engines will be operating at maximum power and they must be monitored carefully.

On the Constellation, there are two set of throttles for powering the engines. One set is located between the pilots and can be used by either the captain or first officer. The other set is behind the pilots and located on the flight engineer's panel. The engineer is primarily responsible for setting the power according to pre-determined propeller rpm and engine manifold pressure. However, the pilots also have to be able to control the power in case of an engine failure or obstruction on the runway requiring the takeoff to be aborted.

Off we go. The captain pushes the throttles forward and tells me to set takeoff power. As the engineer, I do not get to look out the window and enjoy the takeoff. I am busy looking at the engine indications of all 4 engines. Since this is training, there are always failures of some sort.

On a normal flight, we do the "After takeoff checklist." Then, after cruise flight, we prepare to land and accomplish the "Landing preliminary checklist." After the landing gear wheels are extended, we do the "Landing final check list." On taxi in, we do the "After landing checklist." Finally, at the gate when all the engines are shut down, we do the "Secure cockpit checklist." In the real world, that may be the first of 4 or 5 more legs to be flown that day. So the whole drill is repeated over and over.

But we really haven't left the ground, we haven't even left the building. After we are proficient at the normal operating procedures, we go into the emergency and abnormal procedures. If the flying public knew all the things that can malfunction on an airliner, it might raise some eyebrows. However, if they also saw how we trained to handle these situations, it would put their mind at ease.

Each aircraft system has its own set of diabolical emergencies. Engine failures and engine fires required immediate attention. Since the engines were primarily run by the flight engineer, he was a busy guy. As I recall, during an engine fire, there were 13 items that the engineer had to accomplish by memory before the checklist was read. In today's world of modern jet aircraft, there are few memory items, and the FAA mandates the use of checklists to insure procedures are done completely and correctly.

Simulator training is very realistic. You really forget that you are in a simulator. An engine fire feels like a real engine fire and the adrenalin flows.This, along with the fact that your performance is being graded, makes for a nerve wracking few hours. A very tight training syllabus is followed. Again, the maximum amount of information in the minimum amount of time. Any extra training periods backs up the simulator for the trainees coming later. After we are trained on all the emergencies, we are given a check ride to determine if we can proceed to the next phase of training.

There is a check and balance system used in our training. When the instructor completes the applicant's training, a check airman will check and verify independently that the trainee is trained and qualified. In other words, we do not want the instructor to check his own product.

14

Unbeknownst to me, the conflict between the flight engineers union and the pilots union was still boiling. Most of my simulator training was given to me by other new hires that were hired only a few months before me. They were still brand new and they were really hired to be pilots. At the end of our simulator training, we were scheduled for the Emergency Review check ride and then released for airplane training. So when I got my Emergency Review check ride from an old time flight engineer, he was trying to make a point that the new hires teaching us were not cutting the mustard. He failed me on something that I was not taught by my new hire instructor. Fair enough, that is how the system is supposed to work.

This failure is not good. I am absolutely busting my butt studying and practicing my flow patterns. I believe that I know everything that I have been taught. However, taking three parts of the ten part written over, and now having "busted" my emergency ride, I was beginning to feel like there was a spotlight on me.

We already lost one of the twenty guys I was hired with. I knew if you get busted out of one airline, there was no hope to get hired with another airline. So I was set up for another training period. Again the instructor signed me off as being proficient. Remember, this extra training is using valuable simulator time. Once again, I am set up for a "Emergency Review" check ride from another old time flight engineer.

You do not just jump into a simulator and start flying. You start with a one hour briefing in a small room adjacent to the simulator. You brief on what the goals are for the period. When I showed up for this briefing, I felt hostility from the checkairman. Maybe he had the "small man" syndrome. Early on, he let it be known that pilots should not be hired as flight engineers. Uh oh! But I got through the oral part of the check ride and we entered the simulator. We completed many of the emergencies and I was feeling some confidence.

One of the procedures that we worked on was dealing with the engine propellers. These were controlled electrically by blade switches. Our flight handbook says that the blade switches must be operating properly before departure. It is black and white in the book. So on my checkride, the check airman gives me a blade switch problem. He asks if I can control the blade using other procedures. I show him how I could do it. He then asks me what will I tell the captain about the inoperative blade switch before we takeoff. My answer is that I will tell the captain that the book says it must be repaired. This enrages the checkairman. He bangs my head with his index finger over and over yelling "Your job is to get this airplane from A to B. You know how to control the blade switches even if they are malfunctioning." Then he asked me again what would I tell the captain. When I gave him the same answer, get it fixed, he walked out of the simulator. I busted another checkride.

Needless to say, I am more than petrified. Maybe this is where my Military Academy training came into play. All I could do is to deal with it, no mommy or daddy to run to. I made an appointment with the manager of Flight Engineer training for the Constellation. His name was Foe Geldersma. When I entered his office, he was with his assistant, a gentleman named Nels Miller. I explained my situation. I did not blame my instructors, I did not blame the checkairmen, I stated that with my lack of experience, the only thing that I could do was to go by the book. These two gentlemen put me at ease and said that is what I should do.

Instead of more training, Nels Miller said he was going to give me a practice emergency ride the following day. He told me to go home and relax and just do my thing. It was like an evaluation ride to see where I was at. The next day, another classmate of mine was in the same boat with me. He was going to get the same thing. Since he was senior to me, he went first. Two hours later, my classmate came out, and I went into the simulator. The two hours went by and we covered most emergencies. I felt pretty good. When the simulator session was over, Nels Miller congratulated me and told me that I had just passed the Emergency Review checkride with flying colors. I was done with simulator training. What a pleasant surprise. What nice men, Nels Miller and Foe Geldersma. Unfortunately, my classmate was unsuccessful. He was terminated that day.

When I look back over 35 years with TWA, I will never forget Foe and Nels. It could have been easy for them to cut the cord and let me go. In talking to them years later when I was a captain, I reminded them of my meeting with them. They said it was my attitude that saved the day. I did not blame anyone, I just wanted to learn and do my job. Knowing how close I came to being let go, albeit unfairly, I decided to to my best to help fellow pilots successfully complete training and checking. My last 13 years with TWA , I did that as Chairman of the ALPA Training and Standards Committee. More on that later.

Now that simulator training was complete, it was off to train on an actual airplane. Our training base was located at a huge airport miles from downtown Kansas City. This airport was not yet used by the airlines, but it would soon become the main airport for Kansas City. In the airplane, we did many of the same things we did in the simulator. Since we had done this in the simulator, the aircraft phase was fairly routine. We did take an FAA checkride and we earned the Flight Engineer Certificate. It was the first of many FAA checkrides that I would take with TWA.

Finally, we are off to flying the real thing. We would fly revenue flights with passengers on board. Of course, checkairmen were with us and watch closely every step of the way. It was not long before I found an unpleasant part of the flight engineer's job. That is checking and verifying the amount of fuel on board the airplane. This required moving a large metal ladder up to the wing. Next, you climb up and get on top of the wing and walk to the fuel cap found on each wing. We would remove the cap and insert a stick that measured the fuel in inches that would be calibrated into gallons. These wings are very slippery. We are taught to take a very large screwdriver with us. If we slip and fall, stick the screwdriver in the wing so as not to fall off. This job was especially unpleasant when it was cold and windy.

Four months and five days after I entered training in Kansas City, I flew my first trip as the only flight engineer on board from JFK to Washington. We made it without incident. The only problem now is that I was based in New York and Sue and I lived in Chicago. For a long time, a friendly crew scheduler arranged flights for me where I would deadhead to and from New York to work my scheduled flights. That would not happen in today's climate.

18

TWA was expanding rapidly. In my third month on the line as a constellation engineer, I was asked by the manager of flight engineers if I would like to go to B-707 flight engineer school. OMG, I barely know what I am doing on the connie. However, the lure of the big jets was too much. I could finally look out the front window on a 707. The problem was that I got a bid back to Chicago as a flight engineer on the connie. My wonderful wife reluctantly agreed to move to New York so that I could fly the 707. Of course, I had to finish training first.

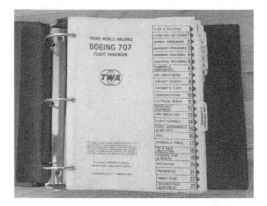

So off I go to 707 school in January of 1965. I was still in my first year probation. How much more can my brain absorb in one year. I did not miss the connie and I enjoyed being in the classroom in the winter. Training on the 707 was light years different from the constellation training. We had state of the art training devices in the classrooms. One of TWA's training innovations kept us awake and alert. Each desk had three buttons with indicator lights attached to them. There were 2 additional lights, one red and one green. The instructors used trays of slides that were projected on the board in the front of class for the different systems. After a few slides, a slide with a question would appear. We would instantly answer with one of the buttons. If you answered it wrong the red light would illuminate and it also showed up at the instructor podium. There was instant feedback and you did not want to get called out by the instructor. Anyway, we all learned from each others mistakes. Again, because of my lack of experience, I was not afraid to ask questions. Many times at the end of class, someone would tell me that they were glad I asked that question.

My 707 classmates were all old time flight engineers. They were grizzled veterans with tons of knowledge. But, like me, they had no jet experience. So I was able to keep up and I eagerly learned what I could. We finished ground school, finished simulator, finished line training, and exactly ten months and six days after I joined TWA, I flew my first flight as a B-707 flight engineer. In ten months I had completed two major courses and earned a flight engineer certificate with ratings to fly reciprocating and turbine powered airplanes. Although I was not actually piloting airplanes, I was gaining invaluable knowledge in airline operations and airplane systems.

While I was in 707 school, my wonderful wife made arrangements to move to New York. However, while I was in school, some 707 flight engineer vacancies opened in Los Angeles. Sue, is it ok if we go to Los Angeles instead of New York? Hollywood! What could be better. Besides, I had a sister living in Los Angeles. Oh yeah, one other thing, we had a baby on the way. I'll bet my in-laws were ready to shoot me. Anyhow, tell the movers we are now going to California.

Once again, it seemed that Lady Luck was watching over me. In order to have insurance cover maternity benefits, you had to be employed with TWA for 10 months. Well, 10 months and 10 days after my start of employment, our daughter Susan arrived on April 25,1965. Of course, I was not there to help, I was in New York. I made it to Chicago for a few days and then I had to leave for my new assignment as a 707 flight engineer in Los Angeles. My mother knew someone who knew someone and somehow I found an apartment in Redondo Beach, about 20 minutes south of the Los Angeles airport.

On May 14, 1965 I worked a flight from Los Angeles to Las Vegas to Chicago and terminated in New York. After a layover in New York, we fly to Philadelphia and Chicago and on to Los Angeles. So on May 15,1965 as we pass through Chicago, I pick up my wife and 19 day old daughter and take them to California. What did I know about raising a child and needing a support system? Sue's mom and dad brought her to the gate at O'Hare and said good-bye. I can not imagine what they must have been thinking.

We arrive in Los Angeles and I am called out to ferry an airplane to Kansas City. At least when I returned, I had about 10 days off. Sue was a real trooper raising our daughter. In Chicago, we had all the medical care we could desire. Now we had to find a baby doctor. Who do we call?

Serving as a flight engineer on the 707 was infinitely more pleasant than on the constellation. The aircraft systems were well designed and our knowledge required to operate the systems did not require us to know how to build it. Switches would make things happen and if they failed to work as advertised, you would go to the book for an alternate procedure. The best part was that I could actually look out the window and watch the pilots fly. I would have paid money just for that.

One captain had a big influence on me. Jerry Boxberger was an exemplary captain and a real gentleman. Even though I had an instrument rating on my pilot license, I really had very little experience in the world of air traffic control. The radio chatter between the controllers and the pilots was crisp and sometimes hard to decipher. Captain Boxberger decided that I should do much of the radio communications while we were in cruise flight. He would tell me what to expect and when to expect it. Okay, this isn't so bad. As I got comfortable, he gave me more rope. On the next leg, he let me call for our routing clearance while we are parked on the ground. This is the important clearance that gives you the entire routing for your flight from takeoff to destination. It must be repeated in the exact

format as it was received. Remember that other pilots from other airlines are listening while waiting in line to receive their clearances. Don't embarrass your airline.

Captain Boxberger was captain on many of my flights. After I became proficient on the radio work, he announced that it was time to see if I could fly the 707. While in cruising flight, Captain Boxberger told me to change seats with the first officer. Before I moved, I made sure that all my flight engineer switches were in the proper place. I eagerly jumped in to the right seat. It took awhile, but I finally adjusted the seat to fit my arms and legs. The airplane was flying on autopilot. A jet airliner is normally flown on autopilot in cruise flight because it is difficult for a pilot to maintain a level altitude because the center of gravity of the airplane keeps changing with people moving around in the cabin. Captain Boxberger disconnected the autopilot, trimmed the airplane for level flight and handed me the controls. You do not fly a jet airliner by looking out the window, you must look at the instruments. I was not worried about the airspeed or heading because they wouldn't change if I did not change the power and kept the wings level. The challenge was to maintain altitude.

Captain Boxberger had me going back and forth between the artificial horizon and the altimeter keeping the wings level and attempting to hold the altitude.

The airplane has a vertical speed indicator that measures your rate of climb or descent in feet per minute. That should not be moving. An even faster indication of change is from the altimeter itself. With the slightest change in altitude, like 10 feet, you make a slight pressure change on the yolk to get the altimeter going back to zero. You do not move the control, you pressure it. At 35,000 feet, being 10 feet off is no big deal. As far as I was concerned,Captain Boxberger could walk on water. It was my good fortune to fly with Jerry Boxberger more than any other captain while I was based in Los Angeles.

As mentioned before, there still was still tension between the flight engineer union and the pilot union. Each union had a separate contract with TWA. Although I would rather be in the first officer seat, the flight engineer pay for a second year employee was significantly higher than 2nd year first officer pay. It was four or five times greater than probationary pay, or what I made at Loyola. Man, I am in high cotton.

In September of 1965, I flew a trip with Captain Paul Rathert who lived in Thousand Oaks, California. He told me of a good buy on a house two doors from him. Sue and I went out and looked at it and decided to buy it. Not a whole lot of thought, we just bought it. Once again, I drag my wife and baby daughter to a place they have never been. That January the rains came and I realized it was safer driving in snowy Chicago than in rainy California. But here we were living the dream!

Since I got hired in June of 1964, TWA has been hiring about 20 pilot crewmen a week. The airline was really expanding. Two classes after my flight engineer class, TWA started hiring new-hires right into the first officer seat. Although I have a seniority number on the TWA pilot first officer list, I cannot use it because I am locked into the flight engineer seat because of the dispute between the two unions. There is no guarantee that I will ever get out of the flight engineer seat. Many of the pilots hired into the first officer seat after me hope guys in my position stay put in the flight engineer seat. They will get bumped backwards when we become first officers.

According to a bill signed by President Kennedy, all old time flight engineers had to earn a Commercial Pilot Certificate with an Instrument rating at TWA's expense. When that was accomplished, they would be given the opportunity to apply for a pilot position. They would keep their seniority number based on the date they were originally hired. Of course, they were all hired years before me. So now it was agreed that the company would start filtering in all the pilot flight engineers into the first officer seats. So instead of hiring first officers off the street, they would go back to hiring flight engineers since there was a supply of first officer trainees in the stream.The company decided on a ratio of 3 or 4 old time engineers for every new hire engineer to go to first officer training. Fortunately, I did not have to wait long. On October 21, 1966 I flew my last trip as a 707 flight engineer, exactly two years to the day that I flew my first tip as a connie engineer. During the two years I spent as a flight engineer, my pilot seniority kept growing. The knowledge and experience that I gained in the flight engineer position was invaluable.

CHAPTER 3

CONVAIR 880 PILOT TRAINING

Sue and I decided to move back to Chicago. The TWA Chicago domicile flew the Convair 880, a sleek 4 engine jet airliner. I was going to transition from a 707 flight engineer to an 880 first officer. Back to school again. Now I am scheduled to go from a single engine light airplane to a heavy 4-engine jet airliner. I hope I get a good instructor.

So here I am back in Kansas City starting my third major training event in a little over two years. A whole new airplane with a different set of numbers and operating limits. The first United States operational supersonic jet bomber capable of Mach 2 flight was the B-58 Hustler built by Convair. Identifying a perceived need for a 4-engine jet airliner that would be both smaller and faster than the the 707 or DC-8, Convair developed its new 880 aircraft incorporating experience gained in the company's production of jet fighters and bombers for the U.S. military. Like the 707 and DC-8, the new Convair 880 also incorporated two jet engines under each sharply swept back wing. The aircraft's cruise speed was planned at 600 mph versus the

560-580 mph planned cruise speed for the 707 and DC-8. Since the speed of 600 mph converts to 880 feet per second, the new aircraft had its model name.

When I showed up at the Kansas City Training Center for First Officer training, I realized I was in for a challenge. The last airplane that I flew as a pilot was a 2,500 pound single-engine, 4 seat propeller airplane that flew at 130 miles per hour. Now I was going to be trained on a 4 engine jet airliner that weighed 184,500 pounds, carried 110 passengers, and flew at 600 miles per hour. My Pilot License did not even have a multiple-engine rating.

Wow! Finally going to sit in one of the front seats!

But first we have to get through Ground School. When we sit down at a desk with a responder board, we are handed a Convair 880 Flight Handbook. It is loose leaf 8 1/2 by 11 that is 3 inches thick and weighs a couple of pounds. It has 23 chapters and looks very intimidating.

Ground school for the 880 is similar that of the 707. Once again, each desk has a responder board. I am impressed with the training methods used by TWA. Ground school is taught by live instructors as opposed to computer based training favored by some airlines. In most cases, the instructor tells you what he is going to tell you, he tells you, and then he tells you what he told you. Then it is your turn to tell what you learned. The aircraft engines and systems are similar between the 707 and the 880. Now I am happy that I had been through the 707 training, at least as far as the systems are concerned. The flying part will be a whole new challenge.

As pilots, we not only fly the airplane, but we must know how all the systems on the airplane work and what to do if they should malfunction. The Convair 880 Flight Handbook deals with Normal Procedures, Non-Normal Procedures, Planning & Performance, Air Conditioning, Aircraft General, Automatic Flight, Communications, Electrical Power, Emergency Equipment, Fire Protection, Flight Controls, Flight Instruments & Air Data, Fuel, Hydraulic Power, Ice & Rain Protection, Landing Gear & Brakes, Navigation, Pneumatics, and Power Plant.

Ground school covers eight 1 hour periods a day and lasts a few weeks. Classes are taught by knowledgeable instructors using slide trays projected on a large screen. After several slides, we are treated with several quiz slides. Again, our responder board answers show up on the instructor's station. It is a great system. If there are too many incorrect answers, it means the instructor failed to teach properly. If one or two students fail to answer correctly, it probably means they were not paying attention. It is embarrassing to get called out by the instructor with an incorrect answer.

After completion of Ground School, there is a 100 question written exam that requires a 90% passing grade. This allows you to enter the Simulator Training Phase. I passed but before I enter the simulator, I better review how an airplane flies.

We all know an airplane has wings. Air flowing over the wings produces lift to make the wings fly. The rear or tail of the airplane has 2 sets of surfaces that help control the wings and stabilize the airplane. One set is another set of smaller wings that are in the same line as the bigger wings. This is called the horizontal stabilizer. The big wings have controls the raise one side of the wing while lowering the other side of the wing. These are called ailerons. The little wings on the tail have controls that make the tail point up or point down to climb or descend. These controls are called elevators. Clever, huh? Attached to the little wings is a control surface called the vertical stabilizer. The vertical stabilizer that sticks up has a control that pushes the tail to the left and to the right. This control is called the rudder. Think of the rudder on a boat that changes the direction of the front of the boat. So the ailerons, elevators, and rudder control the flight path of the airplane while the engine powers it through the air. Got that?

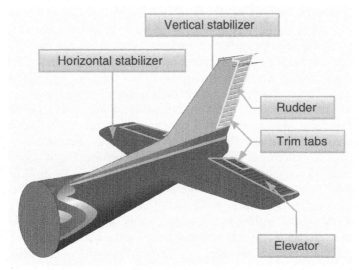

In the 1960s, flight simulators were very simple. The cockpits and instruments were just like the real airplane, but the visual systems displayed to the pilots when the simulator was in motion were not very accurate. They were great for learning checklists, both normal and non-normal, along with many basic flight maneuvers.

So the first thing we have to learn is how to take off. Remember that this airplane that flies at 600 MPH starts out at 0 MPH. Bernoulli's principle says that as air speeds up the pressure is lowered. A wing generates lift because the air goes faster over the top of the wing creating a low pressure that lifts the wing. To make the wing bigger and therefore produce more lift at slower takeoff speeds, the rear of the wing has flaps installed that are extended during take off. These same flaps that are used in slow speed create drag at high speed, so they are retracted as the speed increases.

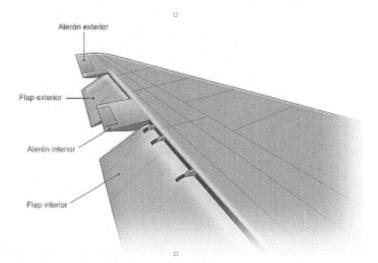

Alerón exterior

Flap exterior

Alerón interior

Flap interior

Ok, back to the simulator. TWA has a strict training syllabus. Our training is expensive and the company does not make money from our services while we are in training. Before each simulator session, the instructor conducts a 90 minute briefing in a small room adjacent to the simulator. It is very thorough. He goes over all that we are expected to cover in the next 4 hours. There are 2 students and we each get to fly the simulator for 2 hours and to observe for 2 hours.

The first session is setting up the cockpit and learning a flow pattern. There are 39 items on the pilot's BEFORE STARTING ENGINES checklist. The checklist is read after all the steps and requirements have been accomplished. The flight engineer has 21 items on his checklist. In the real world, at some time the first officer has to call the tower to get air traffic control clearance for the routing to destination. This can sometimes be daunting at a busy airport like ORD.

NORMAL **880** CHECK LIST

PILOTS   ENGINEER
BEFORE STARTING ENGINES
AT THROUGH STATIONS (NO MECH. DELAY OR CREW CHANGE), NECESSARY TO READ ONLY BOXED ITEMS

Pilots	
1.	GEAR LEVER & LIGHTS .... DOWN & CK
2.	PARKING BRAKE .... ON
3.	BRAKE PRESSURE .... CK
4.	ALTIMETERS & CLOCKS ..... SET & CROSS CK
5.	FLIGHT INSTRUMENTS .... CK
6.	RADAR & TRANSPONDER .... STANDBY
7.	FIRE CONTROLS .... CK
8.	RADIOS .... ON & CK
9.	COMPASSES .... SYNC & SLAVE
10.	WINDSHIELD HEAT .... ANTI-FOG
11.	EMERGENCY EXIT LIGHTS .... OFF
12.	EXTERIOR LIGHTS .... CK
13.	BETA BOX .... CK
14.	NOSE BRAKE SWITCH .... NORMAL
15.	EMERGENCY BRAKE PRESSURE .... CK
16.	EMERGENCY BRAKES .... OFF
17.	STATIC SELECTORS .... NORMAL
18.	AUX EQUIP SELECTOR .... ON
19.	FLAP HANDLE .... SYNC
20.	AUX PUMP & HYDRAULIC PRESSURES...... CK
21.	KIFIS & SPEED STABILITY .... CK
22.	FLIGHT INSTRUMENT SELECTORS .. ALL NO. 1
23.	V$_{mo}$ WARNING .... CK
24.	DRAG BRAKE LEVER .... NORMAL DET
25.	SPOILER SELECTOR .... NORMAL
26.	SPOILERS .... DOWN
27.	AUTOPILOT .... CK & OFF
28.	FLIGHT DIRECTORS .... CK & SCAT
29.	STABILIZER CONTROL ...... CK & NORMAL
30.	TRIM TABS .... CK
31.	EMERGENCY GEAR RELEASES ...... STOWED
32.	ESSENTIAL BUS SEL .... EXT PWR
33.	ISOLATION SWITCHES .... AUTO
34.	ENGINE & WING ANTI-ICE .... CK & OFF
35.	IGNITION SELECTOR .... BOTH
36.	NO SMOKING .... ON
37.	ANTI-SKID .... CK & ON
38.	WARNING LIGHTS .... CK
39.	OXYGEN MASK & REGULATOR CK & SET

Engineer	
1.	BATTERY .... NORMAL
2.	LOAD REDUCTION SWITCHES .... CK & ON
3.	OIL QUANTITY .... CK
4.	FUEL QUANTITY ....
5.	FUEL PANEL .... CK & SET
6.	AIR CONDITIONING PANEL .... CK & SET
7.	PRESSURIZATION CONTROLS ..... AUTO & SET
8.	EQUIPMENT COOLING .... FAN ON
9.	HYDRAULIC QUANTITY .... CK
10.	OXYGEN SYSTEM .... ON & CK
11.	CIRCUIT BREAKERS & LIMITERS .... CK
12.	DC POWER .... CK
13.	26V POWER .... CK & ON MAIN
14.	EMERGENCY INVERTER .... OFF
15.	GENERATOR CONTROLS .... CK
16.	JETTISON & SCAVENGE SWS .... CLOSED
17.	ALT PRESS SOURCES .... CLOSED
18.	TURBOCOMPRESSORS .... OFF
19.	ENGINE HYDRAULIC PUMPS............ ON
20.	OXYGEN MASK & REGULATOR ...... CK & SET
21.	GEAR PINS .... REMOVED

Next the engines are started with a co-ordinated effort by the pilots and the flight engineer. The AFTER STARTING ENGINES checklist is accomplished and the aircraft is ready to taxi.

NORMAL **880** CHECK LIST

PILOTS   ENGINEER

──────────────────────────── TAXI ────────────────────

1. FLAPS .... INDICATE 20^{0}
2. SCAT .... CK
3. PITOT HEATERS .... ON
4. ENGINE ANTI-ICE .... _____
5. STABILIZER TRIM .... SET & CROSS CK
6. T.O. DATA/AIRSPEED BUGS ... SET & CROSS CK

There are 6 items on the TAXI CHECKLIST. Although all the items are important, the first and the last are the most important. The first is FLAPS. The Take Off flaps are required to provide additional lift during the slower aircraft speed during take off. There have been several fatal airline accidents caused by not having the flaps extended for take off.

The last item is T/O DATA/AIRSPEED BUGS. This is going to require some explanation. At this point, I do not have a multi-engine rating on my pilot license and I have no experience flying a multi-engine airplane. So what is the big deal? Simply put, if you lose power during takeoff from an engine failure on one wing, the other wing is producing more engine power and it will want to turn the aircraft toward the direction of the underpowered wing. This is called asymmetric thrust. The aircraft rudder is located in the tail section of the aircraft. This turning tendency on the ground will require the pilot to apply pressure on the rudder with his feet to keep the aircraft going straight on the runway. This is a tricky time and the pilot has to decide whether to stop the airplane or to continue the takeoff. If the engine fails early in the takeoff, the pilot can apply full braking and stop the airplane safely on the remaining runway. If the failure occurs late in the takeoff and there is not enough runway to stop, the aircraft must continue the takeoff using the remaining runway. All these calculations, based on runway length, weight, airport altitude, temperature and flap configuration, are determined before takeoff.

32

So the speed that would come first in the takeoff is called V1. V1 is the engine failure recognition or takeoff decision speed. If the engine fails before V1, you must stop. If the engine fails after V1, the takeoff must continue because there is not enough runway remaining to safely stop. Either one requires some fancy footwork from the pilot.

So if the engine fails after V1, the pilot must continue the takeoff using rudder pressure from one foot to keep the aircraft going straight on the runway until it reaches flying speed. This can be very challenging. That flying speed is called V2. V2 is the speed at which the aircraft may be climbed safely with one engine inoperative. V2 is called takeoff safety speed.

Obviously the airspeed indicator is an important instrument during takeoff. Since V1 and V2 vary with each takeoff, there are movable markers on the outside of airspeed indicator that can be set at the V1 and V2 speeds along with other speeds like flap retraction speeds. These and other markers are called AIRSPEED BUGS.

The time to fly the simulator finally arrives. My simulator instructor was great. He was a TWA pilot that was not on flying status because of a medical problem. His attitude was great and he did not care that I was a low time single engine civilian pilot. He was there to train me and he started with the basics. You fly a jet airliner by looking at the instruments, not by looking out the window as you do flying a light airplane. He taught me a scan pattern, just like I did for my Instrument Rating, that stayed with me for the rest of my flying career. He would have me look at the artificial horizon instrument located in the center of the instruments keeping the wings level. Then I would look at the airspeed indicator and then back to the artificial horizon. Next look at the altimeter and immediately back to the artificial horizon. Next to the heading indicator and back to the horizon. If the wings were still level, I know the heading did not change, the altitude did not change, and the airspeed did not change. He also taught me how to pressure the controls instead of moving the controls. Smooth.

The Convair 880 simulator of the 1960's was not very sophisticated. It could be used for basic instrument flying, several approaches, and an ILS to only one runway. Not very good for engine failures on takeoff and visual landings. That training would be done in the actual airplane.

33

Seven simulator periods in nine days and I was released to aircraft transition training. Once again, there were seven flight training periods scheduled with two at night. Once again, I was fortunate to get a great instructor. He gave me confidence and I was really excited to be actually taking off and landing a 4 engine jet airliner by myself. The aircraft transition training was completed on schedule and the Training Center released me to the Chicago domicile as a first officer.

TWA had six pilot domiciles, each with a management structure. The chief pilot was called the General Manager of Flying, or the GMF. Under the GMF, there was a Manager of Pilots. These two pilots spent much of their time in the office. Next came a couple of Flight Managers that overlooked several Line Check Pilots.

Each domicile is responsible for flying certain flights. The flights are grouped together in a sequence that could go for one to four days. The sequence of flights was called a pairing. Crew schedulers would group several parings together each month into what was called a line of time. The lines were printed on a sheet of paper and listed numerically. This is where seniority counts. The senior captain picks his line and it is removed from choice. The next senior captain gets his choice of the remaining lines. And so it goes for the first officers, and flight engineers. If you were not awarded a line of time, you were assigned to be a reserve pilot. The term "Flying the Line" came to mean you were a pilot flying a line of scheduled pairings..

Even though I was a brand new first officer, I had relatively good seniority because I had been restricted to the flight engineer seat while many first officers were hired after me. So I was awarded a line of time with a pairing that had a layover in Las Vegas for 33 hours. Since I was a new first officer in Chicago, I did not know the captains and they did not know me. So two and a half years after I was hired, I am finally going to fly my first flight as a first officer. I hope I get a nice captain.

However, before we takeoff, we have to prepare the airplane for flight. This is called flight planning. Let's plan a TWA flight from Chicago to Oakland on a Convair 880. Long before the flight crew arrives one hour before scheduled take off time, the TWA Dispatch office is working on the flight plan. Each airline flight in the U.S. is governed by regulations from the Federal Aviation Agency. The main thing determined by the dispatcher is the required fuel to be on board the flight at take off, and this is determined by the distance of the flight and the weather at both ends of the flight.

The dispatcher knows the fuel used on an 880 flight from ORD to OAK. We start with that fuel and add an additional 45 minutes of fuel for reserve. If there is bad weather, we have to add fuel in case we have to hold and then divert to an alternate airport.

OK. There is more to this. The fuel burned is measured in pounds instead of gallons. The 880 has a maximum takeoff weight and a maximum landing weight measured in pounds. So the 880 has a basic operating weight that includes the crew and operating items. We add the weight of the passengers and baggage which is called payload. Then we add the weight of the fuel required for the flight. The total weight cannot exceed the Maximum Takeoff Weight. Subtracting the weight of the fuel burned during the flight cannot exceed the Maximum Landing Weight.

So when the captain arrives, he receives a bunch of papers required for the flight to OAK. The first page is the Dispatch Release. This is the official release from the certified dispatcher that includes the flight number, departure airport, required alternates, destination airport and the fuel required for the flight. It must be signed by the captain to be legal. Before signing, the captain reviews the weather with the first officer. If necessary, the captain may make a phone call to talk to the dispatcher directly. The captain may request an increase in the fuel load. Keep in mind that more weight in fuel is going to mean more fuel is burned in order to carry the additional weight of fuel. The dispatcher and the captain must agree on the fuel load.

Another duty for the first officer is to prepare a flight plan for the flight from ORD to OAK. If the captain was not there, the first officer would pick a route, usually a standard route, using government depicted airways that flew over radio beacons. The first officer had to compute the time used between the beacons using forecast winds aloft. This is how the time and the fuel to the destination was determined. Many times the

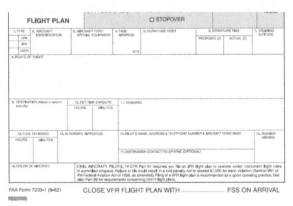

35

captain would chose a different route and everything had to be computed again. With the captains approval, the company would then file a flight plan with ATC for the routing to the destination.

Since it is my first flight I show up early. When the captain shows up, he seems to be very jolly and in a good mood. I did not know it at the time, but he had recently left his position of Manager of Pilots and this was his first trip back as a line pilot. I let him know that this was my initial flight as a first officer. He flew all four legs on the pairing so that I could learn my duties as a first officer.

After 4 days off, we flew the same pairing again. The captain flew the first two legs and let me fly the leg from LAS to OAK. My first landing and I didn't scare the captain and the airplane was still able to fly to ORD. What a thrill. The next trip I got to fly to LAS. I loved flying with Captain John Richey.

The senior pairings had longer legs and less takeoffs and landings than the more junior pairings. After 6 months of flying the line, I only had 46 takeoffs and landings. I wanted to fly pairings that had more legs. In July, I flew a pairing with Captain Norm Lehocky. He flew to Columbus and I flew to Pittsburg. He flew to New York. The next leg was a very short flight from New York to Boston where the weather was at the lowest level allowed for landing. Captain Lehocky said it was my turn to fly the leg. I hand flew the airplane most of the short trip and was allowed to hand fly the ILS instrument approach to the lowest minimums allowed for landing at Boston. It went well and instantly I had another favorite captain.

CAPTAIN UPGRADE TRAINING

TWA was expanding rapidly and pilots in my seniority were starting to be trained as captains. In my opinion, TWA had the toughest captain training in the industry. It was up or out. You either upgraded to captain or you were terminated. The final decision made by the check pilot is if he would put his family on this captain's flight. The failure rate at that time was about 20%. The first step in upgrading to captain is obtaining an FAA Type Rating on the airplane. Back to Kansas City and hours in the simulator and airplane. It takes about 2 months to earn the FAA type rating. Earning the type rating does not make you a TWA captain, it just means you have been approved by the FAA.

At TWA, the real training and testing to become a captain is done flying passenger flights under the careful observation of a line check pilot. Line check pilots flew regular schedules. It became important to me to fly with as many check pilots as possible. I started trading trips with other first officers that were scheduled to fly with check pilots. They were more than happy to trade with me. I traded into a 2 day trip with a check pilot nicknamed "Captain McNasty." He knew I wanted to fly with him. The trip had 9 legs in two days; Chicago to Wichita to Amarillo to Albuquerque to Los Angeles to San Francisco to Las Vegas to Chicago to Baltimore and back to Chicago. I flew all but 2 of the legs. I enjoyed and learned from the trip because "Captain McNasty" not only looked at my flying skills, but he wanted to look at my thinking and situational awareness. This was a really valuable experience from another highly regarded captain.

So after one year and 14 days flying as a first officer, I was told by the company that I was going to Captain Upgrade Training on the Convair 880. This was up or out and I knew I had a lot to prove and learn. Back to Kansas City to earn the coveted FAA Convair 880 type rating. Once again, ground school, simulator, and flight training.

This ground school was going to be different. Not only was the written test required to get out of ground school, a two hour oral exam would be administered by an FAA inspector. This oral exam would cover all normal procedures, non-normal procedures, and all 22 chapters of the Flight Handbook.

Why do we have to know so much about the mechanics of the airplane? I want to fly it, not build it. Well, obviously there are good reasons. Airplanes are made up of many thousands of parts that may be put together by the lowest bidder. When something malfunctions during flight, flight crews write it up in the aircraft maintenance log book so that it can be fixed before the next flight. Sometimes this requires confrontation between the captain and the maintenance department. Some things we can live with and some things we can not fly with. It is up to the captain to know the systems so that he can decide if it is safe or not.

Well I guess that next to the wings, the most important parts of the airplane are the engines. Ok, since I will be flying a jet powered airliner, how does a jet engine work?

Compared to a piston powered engine, a jet engine is a work of simplicity. A jet engine is also called turbine powered. That is because the engine has a shaft down the center of the engine with turbine blades attached to the rear end of the shaft. The front of the shaft has attached compressor blades. In between the compressor blades and the turbine blades is a section called the combustion section. So if the turbine blades are rotating, so are the compressor blades since they are all attached to the same shaft.

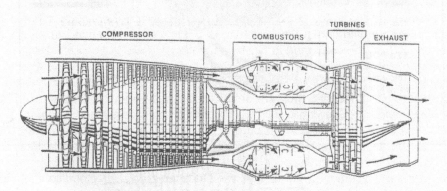

Air enters the front of the engine through the spinning compressor blades. These blades squeeze the air increasing the pressure and temperature of the air. As the air is forced into the combustion chamber, fuel from the aircraft's fuel tank in the wing is added to the compressed air. This mixture is ignited creating a chemical reaction called combustion that burns fiercely giving off hot exhaust gases. The hot exhaust gases rush past the turbine blades spinning them like a windmill. So as the turbine blades spin, they also spin or turn the compressor blades. The hot exhaust gases exit the engine at over twice the speed of the air that entered the engine. The backward-moving exhaust gases power the jet forward. This is called thrust. Neat system!

To start the engine, the trick is to get the turbine blades spinning. You do this by pumping air from a ground air cart outside the aircraft into the compressor blades making them spin that makes the turbines spin at the same time. At a certain rotation speed, fuel and ignition are added to the air compressed by the spinning compressor blades creating combustion. Once the engine is started, the more fuel you add, the more hot gas is pushed through the turbine blades spinning the compressor blades faster. This produces more compressed air for the fuel and ignition to produce more thrust. The more fuel that is added, the more thrust is produced.

One of the major systems on the airplane is the electrical system. I didn't learn much about electricity at the university where I studied biological science. Well there is Direct Current DC electricity and Alternating Current AC electricity. AC is much more powerful and can be produced by generators while DC is mostly produced by lower powered batteries.

AC powers many heavy load items on the airplane such as pumps that move fuel, window heat, power to operate the ovens in the gallery, landing lights, lavatory flush motors, instrument lightening and gauges, shaver outlet, and on and on. When the engines are running, electrical generators are driven by the engine and provide electrical power to distribution points called busses. The busses then supply electrical power to the many items calling for it. DC power is lower power generally used to power warning lights and small valves. DC can be changed to AC by an inverter and AC can be converted to DC by a rectifier.

Another major system is the hydraulic system. Hydraulics are used on aircraft to actuate large heavy items like landing gears, wing flaps, and aircraft brakes. Hydraulics are used because they are able to transmit a very high pressure or force with a small amount of hydraulic fluid that has been compressed by a pump. The power to the hydraulic pump comes from the engine and can also be supplied electrically. Jet airliners have several hydraulic systems so that a single hydraulic system failure is not catastrophic.

There are many other systems that we study including Air Conditioning, both heating and cooling, Fire Protection, Ice and Rain Protection, Emergency Equipment, Flight Controls, Communications, Navigation, Landing Gear & Brakes, and Power Plant. Of course we have to know everything in the TWA Flight Operations Policy Manual and all the Federal Aviation Regulations, especially those concerning Scheduled Airline Operations. Most of the aircraft systems are controlled by the flight engineer.

After two weeks of ground school, I successfully passed the written test and the FAA oral. I was released to the simulator.

My simulator partner was hired after I was but he was hired as a first officer. So he had substantially more time flying TWA airplanes than I did. He was a great partner and we worked well together. During my scheduled 2 hours in the captain's left seat, my partner sat in the right seat and acted as the first officer. After 2 hours we would switch seats and repeat the same procedures. We would have a 90 minute brief before the simulator followed by at least a 30 de-brief after the simulator session.

Once again, the 880 simulator in 1968 was not nearly as realistic as in the modern simulators of the 21st century. Because of this, the meat of the training was conducted in the real airplane at the Mid-Continent Airport in Kansas City.

Wow, I lucked out with a great instructor. He was the same instructor that I had for first officer training. However, this was captain training that included 2 very dangerous maneuvers unique to the Convair 880. First off, we talked about wing flaps that are extended at the trailing edge of the wing flaps that help with lift at lower speeds. The Boeing 707 and Douglas DC-8 also have wing flaps on the front or leading edge of the wings that give more lift a slower speed during takeoff and landing. The 880 does not have these leading edge wing flaps so it requires a longer time on the ground to reach take off speed. This is going to affect take off decision speed (V1) for an engine failure and takeoff safety speed (V2).

When there is an engine failure during take off, the rudder in the tail section of the aircraft helps keep the aircraft going straight down the runway during acceleration. Well, the Convair 880 was designed with a rudder that was not big enough to keep the aircraft going straight down the runway during an engine failure. The FAA gave Convair a break and certified the 880 to leave the runway centerline by 75 feet during an engine failure on takeoff. That is half the width of the runway. So an 880 engine failure during takeoff is a challenging and dangerous maneuver.

The next challenging and dangerous maneuver on the 880 is the 2-engine inoperative approach. Two engines work on one wing and zero engines operate on the other wing. So all the power is on one side of the airplane with no power on the other side. This is called asymmetric thrust. The flight control we use to keep the airplane going straight with engines inoperative is the rudder in the tail section. The rudder controls are controlled and operated by the left and right feet. If both engines are operating on the right wing and no engines are operating on the left wing, the right wing wants to turn toward the left wing. The pilot wants to go straight so he exerts pressure on the right rudder using his right leg and foot. This requires considerable leg pressure. This pressure can be reduced by using the rudder trim knob. The three  flight controls, the ailerons for controlling the wings in turns, the rudder for controlling the nose, and the elevators for climbing and descending, have trim tabs to keep the aircraft in balance. When one or more engines are inoperative, it is extremely important to have all the flight controls in trim where the airplane will fly in balance without pilot input. This reduces the pilot work load and makes the airplane easier to control.

To safely land the airplane with inoperative engines, the pilot has to turn and descend. You descend by reducing the power and using the elevator controls. When the power is reduced, the pressure required on the rudder is also reduced. This requires an input from the pilot. When power is added to slow or stop the descent, pressure to the rudder is increased again. This all can occur while the pilot is turning the aircraft using other flight controls. This can take some pretty fancy flying.

So what is the difference between a normal landing with all engines operating and a 2-engine inoperative landing. With all engines operating, the aircraft is put in the landing configuration, landing gear down and full landing flaps, about 1500 feet above the airport and 5 miles from the runway. You start down descending about 700 feet per minute at a steady landing speed maintained by a steady power on all 4 engines. When over the runway touchdown zone, the pilot gently reduces the sink rate while reducing the engine power. A good approach generally results in a smooth landing.

With the 2 engine approach, the landing gear and approach flaps are lowered much closer to the landing runway. Lowering the landing gear and flaps creates drag on the aircraft requiring large changes in engine power along with fancy foot work. When the landing is assured, the pilot adds landing flaps increasing the drag and requiring more power. It seems to work better when the aircraft is flown onto the runway before reducing power. When the power is reduced for landing, it is helpful to have the flight engineer center the rudder trim control to compensate for the less rudder pressure to keep the airplane going straight ahead. This is a no nonsense maneuver that has no room for error. It would have helped if the FAA would have certified the Convair 880 with a larger rudder.

41

In March of 1968, I earned my FAA Airline Transport Pilot Type Rating for the Convair 880 during a flight test that checked normal operations and emergency operations. It included an engine failure on take off, 2-engine inoperative approach and landing, holding, steep turns, and multiple approaches and landings. The test was administered by an FAA Inspector in the observer seat in the cockpit. My instructor pilot was in the right seat while I flew the aircraft from the left seat. Back on the ground in the flight de-briefing office, while the FAA Inspector was issuing my new pilot license, I realized the FAA recognized me as a captain, but this was only the first step to becoming a TWA captain.

The real captain upgrade approval occurred on actual passenger flights under the careful observation of check pilots. This is make or break time.

The TWA line checking curriculum called for flying a month or 70 hours with a check pilot. If you passed, he recommended that you fly the next month or 70 hours with a different check pilot. If this check pilot approved, you were recommended to take a Semi-final check ride with a management check pilot. If the Semi-final ride was approved, you took the Final check ride with the Chief pilot or the Manager of Pilots. Once again, at TWA, you either passed or you were terminated. Pretty scary for a guy that has only a little over a year as a first officer. This is not a rubber stamp program, I was in for a very close examination.

A distinguished looking Captain Al Lusk was my first check pilot. Right off the bat, one of the biggest difference between the right seat and the left seat is the left seat has a wheel used for steering the airplane on the ground. Holy Smokes, how do I know where to go? Who do I follow? There isn't a gas pedal for driving on the ground. You have to use the jet engines attached to the wings to make the airplane move. Those engines can do a lot of damage to ground equipment with excessive jet blast. I hope I don't hurt anything. This is on the job training.

O'Hare was the busiest airport in the world. How many taxiways are there? Too many. Taxiways are labeled according to the phonetic alphabet, for example, Taxiway Alpha or Taxiway Bravo. Each taxiway can have multiple intersections that are numbered.

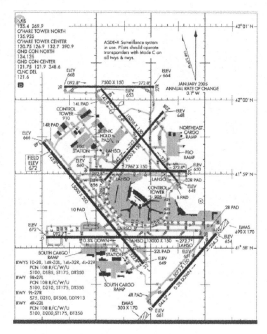

42

At O'hare, Taxiway Alpha has intersections A1 to A21. Each runway has its own parallel taxiway with a designation along with taxiway exit numbers. The airport control tower has controllers that deal with aircraft on the ground and another set of controllers that deals with aircraft taking off and landing.

The ground controller gives us 2 clearances. The first is our airways routing clearance to our destination. This verifies the route and altitude we filed in our flight plan to the destination airport. Once we are ready to depart the gate and taxi, the ground controller clears us to a runway using very specific instructions. We learn ahead of time what the wind is and what runways are in use by listening on the radio to ATIS. This stands for Airport Terminal Information Service. I look at the taxi-way chart and hope I get an easy route to the departure runway.

So my first flight with passengers is from O'Hare to Kansas City. Kansas City has a really short runway for landing but I can't worry about that yet. First I have to leave the gate area and find the takeoff runway. After the passengers are boarded and the doors shut, it is time to start the engines. The three cockpit crew members and a maintenance person on the ground are required to start the engines. The ground person checks to verify there is no equipment or personal near the engines. After the engines are started and we have done the AFTER STARTING ENGINES checklist, the aircraft is pushed away from the gate by a ground cart. He pushes us into an alleyway and points us toward the taxiway. After he disconnects the ground cart, we call for taxi clearance. Once clearance is received, it is time to move the airplane. So I add power gently and slowly, probably too slowly for the check pilot, and the airplane starts to move. Ok, now that we are moving, I want to know how the brakes feel. Believe me, it you hit the brakes too hard, it is very un-nerving for the passengers and the check pilot.

The Convair 880 has 4 wing flap settings: 20 30 40 50. Flaps 20 are used for takeoff as they provide lift. During taxi to the takeoff runway, we run the TAXI checklist which insures that the flaps are set at 20 and the airspeed BUGS are set at V1 and V2.

At the runway departure end, we alert the flight attendants and do the BEFORE TAKEOFF checklist. So here we go, down the runway for a normal takeoff. For pilots, this is an awesome experience. I push the 4 thrust levers forward to a target setting and command the flight engineer to set the thrust evenly on all 4 engines. I am ready and alert to retard the thrust levers if there is an engine failure before V1. At lift off speed we rotate smoothly to initial climb attitude of about 15 degrees nose up. When a positive rate of climb is assured and at takeoff safety speed, we raise the landing gear. Above 800 feet the flaps may be retracted when the airspeed is V2 plus 30 knots. At 3,000 feet  we accelerate to departure climb speed and set the thrust levers to climb thrust.

Next is the AFTER TAKEOFF checklist and we climb to cruising altitude and fly the route to Kansas City. Nearing Kansas City, we do the LANDING PRELIMINARY checklist that prepares the passengers and crew for landing. There is a very important airspeed that is determined before landing. It is called the reference landing speed or VREF. It is based on the landing weight of the aircraft. VREF is computed to be 1.3 X stalling speed with the landing gear down and full landing flaps. A marking is put on the airspeed indicator for the approach and landing and is called a BUG speed.

The Kansas City Airport has only one runway used by jets and it is very short. The approach requires flying over and very close to the RUDY-PATRICK SEEDS building. During the approach, ATC can request that you fly at certain speeds based on other traffic. Slowing down and descending at the same time requires planning and configuring the aircraft using flaps. Once flaps are extended, the airspeed must be monitored carefully to avoid nearing the wing stalling speed. So with FLAPS 20 we need to fly at BUG + 30 kts. FLAPS 30 we can slow to BUG + 20 kts. Next we lower the landing gear and go to FLAPS 40 BUG + 10 kts. After the gear is down, the LANDING FINAL checklist is completed. On final approach between 800 to 500 feet, go to FLAPS 50 BUG + 5 kts. This is fun. Aim at a touchdown target that is 1000 feet down the runway. Once you are over the runway, you no longer look at the landing target on the runway. You look at the far end of the runway to judge your sink rate and adjust it to stop descending. Pull the throttles back and wait for the aircraft to gently touch down on the runway. At least you hope it does.

We land safely and while taxiing to the arrival gate, we do the AFTER LANDING checklist. Kansas City has only one runway and it is easy to find the passenger gates. After engine shutdown at the gate, we do the SECURE COCKPIT checklist. Whew!!

We have about an hour before we fly the next leg to Las Vegas. Captain Lusk and I go into the TWA ramp office to look over the weather and the flight plan. Again, he was a gentleman and acted as if it was a routine flight. So I must say that I enjoy flying from the left seat and acting like a captain. With Captain Lusk, I flew a total of 35 legs, ranging from 26 minutes to 2 hours and 33 minutes. During many of the flights, we would discuss different situations I might be confronted with as a captain. Several times he asked me where I would plan to go if I experienced an engine failure. He also wanted to know the reason behind my decisions. He was a pleasure to fly with and he recommended that I continue with the next check pilot.

The following month, I was going to be checked and graded by a captain that I admired and respected greatly. He was Captain Jack Wooden, a B-17 pilot from World War II. We flew 51 legs together ranging from 32 minutes to 3 hours and 36 minutes. Captain Wooden had me relaxed and I flew almost all of the legs. This was valuable training even though I knew I was being graded. My confidence level grew along with experience gained while taxiing on the ground at multiple airports. Captain Wooden shook my hand and recommended that I take the Semi-Final Check Ride.

The Semi-Final Check Ride is a validation and verification of the recommendations for my previous check pilots. It was 6 leg trip over 2 days administered by the Chicago Manager of Pilots, Captain Harry Jacobson. No doubt I was nervous and realized I was getting closer to the end. Captain Jacobson approved and I was recommended to take the Final Check Ride.

My Final Check Ride was conducted by the Chicago General Manager of Flying, the Chief Pilot, Captain Jack Robertson. Walking to the airplane, Captain Robertson complimented me on the way I wore my hat and buttoned my uniform. He liked things like how you looked. It was a 2 day trip with 6 legs and a layover in Kansas City. I stayed in my hotel room the entire layover. The last day we flew from Kansas City to Los Angeles to Denver, and on to Chicago. I flew all 3 legs and after parking at the gate, Captain Robertson invited me to his office for congratulations. Truly, one of the most memorable moments of my life. Pre-

med college student to captain on a 4-engine jet airliner on one of the world's premier airlines. An unlikely journey in which a lot of things had to go right. On August 31, 1968, Captain Robertson said to me, "Jerry, we made you a TWA captain. Now go out and act like one."

It wasn't long before I flew my first trip as captain. It was scheduled from Chicago to Philadelphia. There was a standing joke the you could not depart until the weight of the required flight documents weighed the same as the airplane. These documents were received in a room under the passenger gates called the ramp office. TWA had many flights in and out of Chicago, so the ramp office was large and was always crowded with crewmembers. It had an attached lounge for the crews with a television set, where the crewmembers shared rumors.

It was the first time I was in the ramp office wearing four stripes, captain wings, and the gold scrambled eggs on my captain's hat. I wasn't strutting around like a peacock, I was concerned about the bad weather in Philadelphia. A new captain has higher landing limits until he accumulates 100 hours as a captain. A senior captain the I admired discussed the situation with me and assured me that if other airplanes were landing, I should plan on landing also. Even though I had just completed the toughest captain upgrade training in the industry, I was wondering if there was something else I should know. Assured by a fellow captain, I flew my maiden flight successfully to Philadelphia.

About a year after flying the line with regular schedules, I was called into the Chief Pilots office who was now Captain Harry Jacobson. He told me that I was being asked to become a Convair 880 instructor pilot at our training center in Kansas City. I was flattered but I told him that I was happy flying the line in Chicago.

It turned out it was not a request. I was to report to Kansas City for training with 3 other new instructors. My boss at the training center was Captain Buck Pratt, the Convair 880 Fleet Manager. Captain Pratt gave me a proficiency check in the airplane with an FAA inspector observing. This was my blessing to become an instructor pilot. Not only could I instruct in the simulator and the airplane, I could conduct Annual Recurrent Training Checks in the simulator. This was fun because I gave a Recurrent Training Check to the Chicago Manager of Pilots, Captain Curt Rogers. He did great but I piled on an engine fire and turbulence just as he was making a complicated entry into a holding pattern. He turned to look at me and asked me what the hell I was doing. I just smiled.

Flight instructing is an incredible learning experience. However, I would prefer to fly the airplane myself rather than watching someone else fly the airplane. After a year, I resigned from the training center and returned to Chicago as a line pilot. The 3 other pilots I reported with spent their entire careers in the training department or in management.

CHAPTER 4

B-707 and B-727

The Boeing 707 was another 4-engine jet airplane that I flew as a captain. TWA had several models of the 707 and they all had their own peculiarities. The 707s were larger than the 880 and had totally different engines. The 707 engine had 2 sets of compressors attached to 2 sets of turbines with the combustion section in between. The 707s were much larger and flew farther.

The training to be a captain on the 707 had changed. The simulator was safer and way cheaper to operate than the actual airplane. After the FAA oral exam, you received part of the FAA Type rating in the simulator. When that was completed, you finished up with a few maneuvers in the airplane.

My 707 oral exam was conducted by an FAA Air Carrier inspector. He seemed surprised and resentful that I was so young training to be a TWA captain on the 707. The oral was conducted in a 707 Cockpit Procedures Trainer or CPT. The CPT has all the instruments and switches of the cockpit but it does not simulate flight. The inspector sat in the flight engineer's seat and I sat in the captain's seat.

Before the FAA oral, I spent a day in the CPT with a ground school instructor who prepped me for the oral. I was advised to miss a question early in the oral so that the inspector could give me the answer and make him feel good. The oral was supposed to be about the 707. My first few questions from the inspector were not about the 707, but they were about FAA regulations. I  could not miss those questions. Then, using his pointer, he asked me about all the instruments and their power sources. I answered them all correctly. When the inspector completed going around the entire cockpit, he said we were done early and we must have missed something. So he started all over from the beginning. After another 35 minutes, he asked me if I knew where the cockpit air shutoff valve was located. This was used for smoke in the cockpit. I had been a flight engineer on the 707 and I knew exactly where it was. I told the inspector that I did not know where the cockpit air shutoff was located. He got out of the flight engineer seat and showed me where it was located. That was the end of the oral. I passed but he would not let me go until I missed a question. This so he could teach me. I was not done with this inspector.

After a few periods of instruction in the simulator, I was set up to take the simulator portion of the FAA of 707 Type rating. This was scheduled with the same FAA inspector that gave me the oral exam. My lucky day. At the inspector's direction, I was given clearance to a holding pattern that required a complicated entry. A standard holding pattern takes about 4 minutes. In training, the instructor normally asks what the initial heading is after crossing the fix into the pattern. This tells him if you are making the correct entry. Then the instructor goes on to another maneuver to save valuable simulator time. Not on this check ride. After entering the holding pattern and hand flying for a few minutes, I put the airplane on autopilot and completed the 4 minute pattern. Then I completed another 4 minute pattern. I knew the inspector was trying to figure out how I got into the holding pattern. After a few more minutes the inspector told the instructor to go on to some other maneuvers. Then abruptly, the inspector told my instructor to put the simulator on the ground. Once on the ground, the inspector told my instructor that I made an incorrect entry into the holding pattern. The instructor explained how I made my entry and why it was the correct entry. This embarrassed the inspector. The inspector then said the checkride was over and that I passed. I believe he intended to fail me if I made the wrong entry. Glad my instructor stood up for me.

The next day I completed the airplane portion of the Type Rating with a real gentleman FAA inspector. Next off to fly the line with passengers.

B-727

Enough of the 4 engine flying. When the 880s were retired, it was time to check-out in the modern 3-engine Boeing 727.   This airplane had several overall improvements that added to its utility. The 727 has multiple leading edge devices on the front of the wing, The 880 did not have these devices. These devices allowed for a much slower approach speed on the 727.

The 707s and the 880 had to use jet ways for boarding and deplaning passengers. The 727 had air stairs at the rear of the airplane that allowed boarding and deplaning without being at a passenger gate. Also, the 727 had an Auxiliary Power Unit or APU. The APU has air power energy to start the aircraft engines without a ground air cart that is required on the 707 and 880. The APU also has an electrical generator to power the electrical needs of the aircraft while it is parked at the gate. Drawing air from its own compressor, the APU drives the Air Cycle Machine

to heat and cool the airplane. So the APU provides air to start the engines, supplies electrical power, and can air-condition the aircraft.

It was a pleasure flying the 727 out of the Chicago domicile. We flew all directions out of Chicago and most of the pairings had many takeoffs and landings which I enjoyed. In addition to recurrent training once a year, captains were required to take a simulator proficiency check 6 months later. So every 6 months we returned to the training center to demonstrate our ability to handle aborted takeoffs, engine failures on takeoff, approaches to stall recovery, steep turns, cross wind landings, engine out landings, multiple landing approaches, missed approaches, engine fires, and many system failures. The 727 was powered by three engines located next to each other in the rear of the airplane. There were no wing mounted engines. So right off the bat, an engine failure during takeoff did not require lots of rudder pressure but you just lost one-third of the power. Captains were also required to complete a TWO ENGINES INOPERATIVE APPROACH and landing. The training center was called Tension Tech where we played Show and Tell.

One of the things I enjoyed while based in Chicago was the meetings conducted by ALPA or the Air Line Pilots Association. ALPA was made up of pilots from all the major airlines except American Airlines. At the time, there were about 33,000 pilot members with each airline having its own representatives. At TWA, each domicile had representatives for the captain, first officer, and flight engineer positions. These three representatives comprised the Local Executive Council or LEC. Each LEC had a number and Chicago was Council 25. The combined representatives of all the TWA LECs made up the Master Executive Council or MEC. While I was a first officer, I volunteered to be on the Professional Standards Committee. this committee dealt with personality conflicts, non-adherence to standard operating procedures, and distracting personal habits. There were very few issues. After representing Council 25 at monthly meetings that allocated flying time assigned to each domicile, I was elected as the captain representative for Council 25. This made me a member of the TWA Master Executive Council and also a member of the National Board of Directors of the Air Line Pilots Association. The

required ALPA meetings were generally very professional but were sometimes downright hostile. Roberts Rules of Order were strictly enforced.

There were two majors issues that I dealt with as the LEC chairman. The first was with the Aeromedical Committee that deals with alcohol and substance abuse. To its credit, I believe TWA was one the first airlines to recognize alcoholism as a disease instead of a crime. This required trust and cooperation between the airline, ALPA, and the affected crewmember. When it was suspected that a crewmember may have an alcohol problem, the company wanted it handled by the ALPA Aeromedical Committee through the LEC chairman. ALPA and TWA had a zero tolerance for flying while under the influence. If you flew and covered for an intoxicated pilot, you were fired and the intoxicated pilots sent to rehab. So we wanted to identify suspected abuse so that we could rehabilitate the crewmember. During my term as LEC chairman, I sent 3 flight crewmembers to the Hazelden Rehab Center in Minnesota. Two were captains and one was a first officer. The two captains successfully completed the program while, unfortunately, the first officer did not and he was terminated.

The next event dealt with a near TWA aircraft catastrophe in flight. The Chicago hief pilot, Captain Harry Jacobson, called me very early on April 5, 1979. He told me nat there was a TWA incident at the airport in Detroit and that we were the closest LPA and management pilots in the area. We met at ORD and flew to Detroit on merican Airlines. When we arrived, I had no clue what had happened but the press vas out in force. It turned out the a TWA Boeing 727 flying over Michigan at 39,000 eet began a sharp, un-commanded roll to the right and subsequently went into a piral dive. The pilots were able to regain control of the aircraft and made a uccessful emergency landing at the Detroit Metropolitan Airport. The pilots were in n airport hotel where I interviewed each individually in separate rooms. Their story f what happened was heroic, chilling, and identical. I wish I could have recorded it, ut for some reason, that was against ALPA policy.

The flight crew and I were notified that there was going to be an initial nvestigation of the incident conducted by the FAA and NTSB at the hotel later that fternoon. My only advice to each crewmember was to tell the truth. Lying to a ederal agent is a crime. After listening to them, I knew they performed heroically, rofessionally and had nothing to hide. At the hearing, I watched Captain Jacobson s Captain Hoot Gibson described the event that I had already heard. Captain acobson's jaw dropped as the event was described by Captain Gibson.

My ALPA role in the incident ended when the chairman of the TWA ALPA Safety committee arrived to represent the flight crew at the hearing. I wish I had stayed nvolved because of a totally bogus outcome. The aircraft was turned over to Boeing or examination. Do you think that Boeing would find something wrong with their irplane? No. They blamed the incident on the flight crew. I know and I am positive nat the flight crew did not cause this near tragedy. Boeing could not afford to shed ad light on their popular 727 model. Captain Gibson passed away years later houldering the burden of being falsely accused of causing a near tragedy.

CHAPTER 5

B-767

The next aircraft that I captained was the twin engine B-767. So I went from 4 engines to 3 engines and now to 2 engines. Is it possible that I could end up on 1 engine? We shall see. The 767 was the first Boeing wide-body to be designed with a two-pilot crew digital glass cockpit. A glass cockpit is an aircraft cockpit that features electronic (digital) flight instrument displays, typically large LCD screens, rather than the traditional style of analog dials and gauges. It displayed the flight path over the ground in the cockpit just like the navigation systems in modern automobiles. New automated electronics replaced the role of the flight engineer by enabling the pilot and co-pilot to monitor aircraft systems directly.

TWA had a policy that if a crewmember was unable to transition from a narrow-body 880, 707, or 727 to a wide-body L-1011 or B-747, that crewmember was restricted to the narrow-body for the remainder of his career. The new B-767 was considered a wide-body aircraft by TWA. A Chicago based captain who was senior to me bid to fly the 767 out of St. Louis. He failed the training to transition to the 767 and was restricted to the 727 for the several years remaining of his career. Well I already had a 747 type rating, so I was not all that concerned.

Back to the Training Center for the worst ground school in my career. This was a new airplane with a new way of navigating, and unfortunately some new ground school instructors were unfamiliar with the new philosophy. The electrical system, hydraulic system, air-conditioning system, fire protection, etc. were all improved Boeing systems. The big change was the navigation and flight instrument displays. This was state of the art and was used in all Boeing aircraft that followed.

The new navigation system was a by-product of NASA research on navigation to the moon. To get to the moon, you could not use radios based on the earth. So they developed the Inertial Reference System (IRS). Each IRS contains a laser gyro which senses attitude change. Each gyro is paired with an accelerometer that senses acceleration along that axis. Tell the IRS where it is on the ground and it senses it's movement in relation to earth and knows where it is in space. Wow! The IRS replaces the conventional compass system.

Next, the IRS presents its position to the Flight Management Computer (FMC). There are two FMCs that can be connected to the autopilots, flight directors, and auto throttles to completely control all lateral navigation (L NAV) and vertical navigation (V NAV) of the aircraft. Previously, we would fly inbound to a radio on a radial and fly outbound on another radial of the same radio. With the new system you only flew inbound to a computer waypoint, not to a radio. This was not well explained by the instructor.

Pilots know the position of the airplane relative to the earth using an attitude indicator instrument. This instrument shows the position of the wings and the nose relative to the earth which is displayed as a brown ball with a blue sky above it. The attitude indicator, the compass, the altimeter, and the airspeed indicator were considered the basic flight instruments. The 767 displayed symbols of those instruments in one glass covered display, thus the glass cockpit.

Boeing's philosophy maintained that the autopilot flies more efficiently than the pilots. Pilots were expected to use the autopilot as much as possible. This troubled me. Why? Every six months, captains are required to take a proficiency check in the simulator or airplane. Maneuvers such as stall recovery, steep turns, emergency descents, visual approaches, non-precision approaches, missed approaches and crosswind landings are all flown manually and are required on the check.

After ground school and the oral exam by an FAA inspector, I started training in the most realistic simulator that I had ever experienced. The TWA 767 simulator artificially re-creates aircraft flight and the environment in which it flies. The visual system is so realistic that the FAA allows pilots to earn the FAA B-767 Type Rating in the simulator. My simulator instructor and I were instructors together on the 880. We finished our first period syllabus early and had time to play with the simulator. My instructor asked what I wanted to do. So I made some visual landings. Then I tried some cross-wind landings. What fun and what a great confidence builder from a great instructor.

B-767
Simulator

One of the most challenging maneuvers is flying the 767 with one of its two engines shut down. As explained on the Convair 880 training, the wing with the power wants to turn toward the wing with no power. Again, this is called asymmetric thrust. The pilot is required to control the rudder with one leg and foot to keep the airplane going straight ahead. An engine failure requires a strong muscular leg effort on the side of the operating engine to keep the rudder in balance. Fortunately the pilot can relieve the pressure on his leg by  applying rudder trim to balance the airplane. Trim tabs are installed on ailerons, elevators and rudders to balance the control surface in flight so the controls felt by the pilot remain in the neutral position without pilot pressure which could result in muscle fatigue.

Having already been FAA Type Rated on the CV-880, B-707 and the B-727, I was disappointed to find out that the engine out procedure on the 767 was markedly different from the other aircraft. On all the other aircraft, the pilot was allowed and expected to use rudder trim during an engine out approach. During an engine inoperative approach on these aircraft, the rudder trim would be removed as the throttle power was reduced for landing and the airplane would stay aligned with the runway.

This was not the case on the B-767. TWA's procedure at the time was to fly around on one engine with rudder trim until arrival at the final approach fix. This was generally 5 miles from the runway and about 1500 feet above the ground. Approaching the final approach fix, 767 pilots were required to remove the rudder trim and use leg muscles to keep the airplane aligned with the runway using the high engine power required during the approach. This means the approach must be flown with an out of trim rudder making the airplane unstable and creating muscle fatigue. Remember, one engine on one side is now doing the work of two engines. When power is reduced on the operating engine to land, some fancy foot work moving the rudder is required to keep the airplane aligned with the runway. I was told the reason for this procedure was that the nose wheel steering was tied to the rudder. That is fine except we touch down on the main landing gear before the nose wheel touches down. After completing my B-767 type rating in the simulator with the FAA, I commented that I would use rudder trim during a real engine out situation because I felt it was safer. Little did I know how soon I would face that situation.

After the simulator training, you receive 25 hours of Initial Operating Experience (IOE) flying the 767 on scheduled passenger flights with a check airman. This is supposed to be a learning experience from the check airman. It is called operating experience. My check airman was junior to me and let me know that he resented the fact that I was transferring from Chicago to St. Louis to fly the 767. The first leg was not instructional but more like a check ride. I was still the MEC Training and Standards Committee Chairman and I told him what I thought of his attitude and methods. My next check airman wasn't much better but I was released to fly the line as a 767 captain.

Finally I was flying the 767 without someone watching me. My first few flights, I hardly ever used the autopilot. Couldn't wait to see how the airplane flew without the autopilot. I might have wasted a little fuel, but I got very comfortable with hand flying the airplane. This was going to come in handy in the not too distant future.

TWA spearheaded the growth of twin-jet 767 flights across the northern Atlantic under extended-range twin-engine operational performance standards (ETOPS) regulations. ETOPS tests include shutting down an engine and flying on the remaining engine to a diversion airport. It must be demonstrated that, during the diversion flight, the flight crew is not unduly burdened by extra workload due to the lost engine and that the probability of the remaining engine failing is extremely remote.

The FAA and ICAO concluded that a properly designed twin-engined airliner can make intercontinental transoceanic flights. TWA was awarded the first ETOPS rating in May 1985 for Boeing 767 service between St. Louis and Frankfurt, Germany allowing TWA to fly its aircraft up to 90 minutes away from the nearest alternate airport.

June 6, 1985 a beautiful summer day in Germany, I was excited to command TWA Flight 745 from Frankfurt to St. Louis. The flying time was scheduled for 9 hours and 27 minutes. Flights over 8 hours required a relief pilot and he was sitting in the cockpit jump seat. There was a full load of passengers and fuel.

ETOPS regulations required our flight to be within 90 minutes of an approved alternate airport in case of an engine malfunction. Our route took us northwest over the Netherlands and the United Kingdom towards Iceland where a suitable alternate airport was located. Several hours into the flight, everything was operating smoothly. In the cockpit, the relief pilot was standing between the pilot seats discussing our international operations. We were about an hour southeast of Iceland over the North Atlantic Ocean when a red emergency light illuminated. It was the left engine oil pressure light indicating the oil pressure was low. We checked the instrument panel and confirmed the the oil pressure indicator showed the pressure was decreasing. The left engine oil quantity gauge indicated Zero. With 2 indications of an oil problem, we are required to shut down the engine.

Shutting down an engine while cruising at 39,000 feet in the middle of the ocean as not on my wish list. The EMERGENCY 767 CHECKLIST procedure for an NGINE FAILURE has 10 steps to be followed. The engine was secured according) standard operating procedures. Although the 767 is able to safely fly on one ngine, the airplane is unable to maintain level flight at higher altitudes and must escend. In order to descend, we must divert off course so as not to interfere with ircraft that may be below us. Our diversion procedure at the time called for a turn off ourse in the direction of the nearest suitable airport.

The axiom "Aviate, Navigate, Communicate" is a reminder of the pilot-in-ommand priorities during emergency situations.

Aviate-Maintain control of the aircraft
Navigate-Know where you are and where you intend to go
Communicate-Let someone know your plans and needs

I disconnected the autopilot and trimmed the rudder for flight on one engine. We escended the airplane and navigated toward Iceland. The non-flying pilot ommunicated with Oceanic control that we were declaring an emergency and escending and diverting to Keflavik, Iceland. We also had to communicate with TWA ispatch to advise them of our emergency. The passengers and flight attendants could tell something was amiss and I advised them of our plans to land in Iceland because of a mechanical problem.

Murphy's law states "Anything that can go wrong, will go wrong." The fact that this flight had an engine shut down, I wanted the flight crew and the cabin crew to mentally prepare for the possibility of an ocean ditching in case the other engine failed.

TWA's training included an engine inoperative ILS approach procedure. The precision ILS is a highly accurate radio signal navigation aid that provides the pilot with both vertical and horizontal guidance when landing in low visibility.

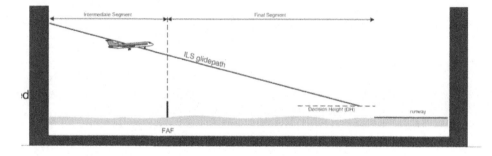

Having demonstrated proficiency in this maneuver only months ago, I was confident of flying a successful single engine ILS approach. Murphy's law was lurking. We were informed that the ILS at Keflavik was shut down for maintenance and was not available. We would have to do a non-precision VOR approach to an altitude below the prescribed safe landing minimums for a VOR approach.

A non-precision approach is a misnomer in that it requires more precision flying because of the lack of vertical guidance that the ILS glide path provides.

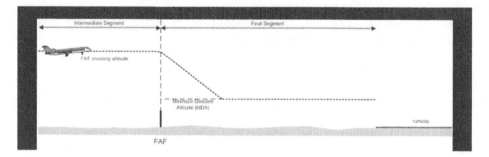

In the 1980s, a non-precision VOR approach was flown as a series of step-down fixes. After reaching one fix, pull the power off and descent to a set altitude and then level off by adding engine thrust until reaching the next fix. At the Final Approach Fix start descent to a Minimum Descent Altitude (MDA) altitude and level off until you see the runway or execute a missed approach. Descent requires reducing power and level off requires adding power and maintaining that power for some distance. Managing the rudder without using rudder trim on a multiple step down approach can be very challenging.

TWA had a published procedure for an engine inoperative landing in good weather. There was also a published engine inoperative procedure for an ILS approach in bad weather. However, there was no procedure for an engine inoperative VOR non-precision approach in bad weather. I discussed my plan with the flight deck crew and informed them of my intention to manually hand fly the entire approach with the required rudder trim and that I would not remove the rudder trim prior to the final approach fix as was called for in training. This was an emergency and I intended to Aviate. I briefed the relief pilot in the jump seat when and how to remove the rudder trim on my command as we landed.

This approach would be far different from a normal approach. The 767-200 was designed without a fuel dumping system which is used to reduce the landing weight of the aircraft. An overweight landing with a higher landing speed was our only choice. Also, the approach has to be flown at a 20 knots higher speed because only partial wing flaps are used because full landing flaps create too much drag and severely limit the aircraft's ability to climb if necessary. This approach speed will be close to 200 MPH. A missed approach was not an alternative since there was nowhere else to go. So we had to get it right the first time.

TWA Flight 745 was cleared for the VOR Runway 20 approach. We crossed the Final Approach Fix at 2300 feet, reduced power to descend to published minimums of 440 feet above the ground and leveled off. Level flight required more engine power and more rudder trim. This was an emergency and using captain's authority I was ignoring the prescribed procedure of removing all rudder trim. At 440 feet above the ground, minimums for the VOR approach, we were still in the clouds and could not see the ground. We descended to 300 feet and started to see some ground. The control tower was watching us on radar. We were below the ILS glide slope and the tower advised us to go around because they thought we were too low. We were right on course holding a level altitude safely above the ground and I told the non-flying pilot to report that we had the field in sight. We did not see the runway but I was confident we would see it soon. We descended to 250 feet above the ground and the runway approach lights came into view. We started down and crossed the end of the runway. As I reduced the power for landing, the relief pilot removed the rudder trim and we made a normal landing using a time tested technique. The rudder was centered and so was the nose steering wheel.

We touched down very fast and I decided to use moderate braking to prevent overheating the brakes and possibly having a tire blowout. We turned off at the end of the runway and began a long taxi back to the airline ramp.

TWA diverted a 747 en route to New York from Athens to Keflavik to to pick up the passengers and cabin crew. The pilots stayed with the aircraft to see if the oil leak could be repaired. It could not, so we deadheaded back to the U.S. on Icelandic Air the following day.

This adventure led to some procedure changes. TWA pilots were advised to hand fly at least one approach on every flight pairing to maintain manual flying proficiency. Also, the requirement to remove all rudder trim prior to the final approach fix was removed. One more change since the Iceland adventure over 30 years ago; the new Boeing 777s and Boeing 787s have automatic rudder compensation during engine out operations. It is called thrust asymmetry compensation. This greatly reduces the work load of the pilot flying the aircraft and most importantly, it keeps the aircraft in proper trim.

Finally, about 7 weeks after the Iceland incident, I received a report detailing the cause of the oil leak. A metal bolt, not part of the 767, was found in the oil system drain pan. The bolt had torn a rubber seal that allowed the oil to leak from the engine. How the bolt got in the drain pan is a mystery. Could it be "Murphy's Law"???

CHAPTER 6

LOCKHEED L-1011

After my Iceland adventure, I trained to be a captain on the Lockheed L-1011 Tristar. Ok, I am moving back up to 3 engines. When Lockheed announced the development of the 3-engine L-1011, McDonnell Douglas developed the DC-10 on a "very firm budget, and cost overruns were unacceptable—even at the expense of safety." By contrast, Lockheed would "take the most advanced technology of the day and when that technology was lacking, Lockheed created it" for the L-1011.

Design problems on the DC-10 resulted in two accidents that could not have happened on the L-1011. Hydraulic lines that controlled the flight controls were installed under the passenger seats on the DC-10. When a cargo door failed and opened inflight, the passenger seats collapsed downward severing the flight controls. Lockheed, on the other hand, installed the hydraulic lines to the flight controls above the passenger seats eliminating the problem.

The leading edge flaps used on takeoff are extended by hydraulic pressure. On the L-1011, once these flaps are extended, it takes hydraulic pressure to retract them. So if hydraulic pressure is lost, the flaps stay extended for safety. A DC-10 lost hydraulic pressure on takeoff causing the leaking edge flaps to retract, This led to a loss of lift and the aircraft crashed with many fatalities

The L-1011 simulator was very realistic. Proficiency check maneuvers included rejected takeoff, engine failure after V1, approaches to stalls, missed approaches, rejected landing, two-engine inoperative landing, and many more. One of the more difficult maneuvers was the approach and landing in a 35 knot crosswind. The nose of the aircraft came in at a very high angle and after the rear wheels were on the ground, I felt it was tricky flying the nose wheel onto the ground.

Taxiing the real airplane took a little getting used to. The nose wheel used for steering on the ground is 30 feet or 10 yards behind the cockpit. Making a 90 degree turn meant you had to go straight ahead of the turn line by 10 yards before turning the aircraft. This took faith in where you thought you were since you had no visual reference.

The L-1011 had a highly advanced autopilot that could be used for ILS approaches is bad weather. There are 3 ILS categories based on visibility seen by the pilots at a designated height above the runway. A Cat I ILS needs a 200 foot decision height and 2600 feet visibility. A Cat II ILS needs a 100 foot decision height and 1200 feet visibility A Cat III ILS requires no decision height and no visibility requirement. The L-1011 was the first wide body to receive FAA certification for Cat III landing performed by the aircraft's autopilot in Cat III visibility weather conditions. This system came in handy on several of my flights.

Charles de Gaulle airport serving Paris is located in a shallow valley that is susceptible to ground fog. In order to use the Cat III auto land system, the captain must be qualified, the airplane must be qualified, and the airport must be qualified. TWA L-1011 captains demonstrate proficiency on these approaches every six months which maintained their qualification. The airplane must have all its autopilot and ILS equipment in working order. Finally, CDG airport has several approaches that qualify for Cat III auto landings in Cat III visibility.

My preference was to hand fly and make a manual landing every chance I had. However, in certain conditions, we were required to use the autopilot for an automatic landing. In the interest of safety, TWA has a no-fault go-around policy. Pilots should

execute every approach with the presumption that a missed-approach is a successful outcome. The captain is under no pressure to land.

Monitoring and watching the autopilot during an auto landing approach is exciting and requires intense concentration on all the instruments. Any single failure requires an immediate missed-approach. Again, because of the high angle of approach when the L-1011 main landing wheels touch the ground, the cockpit is still 30 feet in the air and possibly still in the fog. Once the nose wheel touches down, the captain has extremely limited forward visibility for taxiing the airplane.

The landing at CDG was made completely hands off. The autopilot kept the plane on the proper course and the auto throttles held the proper speed. On touchdown the rudder and nose wheel keep the airplane on the runway centerline and the auto brakes and engine reverse slow the airplane until the captain disconnects the auto systems and takes control of the aircraft. Now the hard part begins. How do we get to the parking gate?

The tower tells us what taxiway turn off we are at since we cannot see the marking. CDG has an awesome taxiway lighting system. It has green lights to follow and red lights where it does not want you to go. As you approach the gate, a person on the ground signals you to stop and another person attaches the jetway to the aircraft. The passengers happily deplane after a long flight.

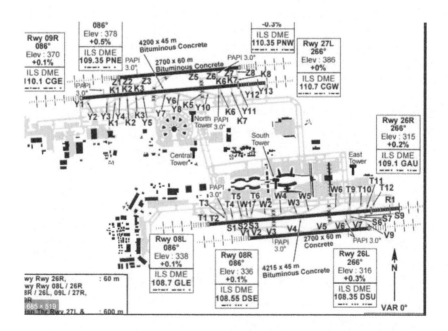

Airline pilots are probably more scrutinized than any other profession. First off, I took an FAA flight physical exam every six months. There was an extensive questionnaire that had to be filled out for the physical exam. Any falsehoods on the questionnaire was a federal offense. The doctor's examination included an EKG, hearing, and a vision test. Also, every six months we were checked in the simulator. One check was with a first officer and flight engineer and we were checked as a crew. The next six month check was for the captain only and it was a pass or fail checkride. OK, once a year you were checked by a TWA check pilot on a passenger flight called a line check. And then there are the flight recorders. They record all the cockpit conversations along with data from the flight of the aircraft. Finally you are subject to an FAA line check at any time by an FAA inspector.

A memorable L-1011 event occurred during a FAA line check I was receiving from the FAA inspector responsible for the TWA L-1011 fleet. He was a large man over 6 feet and could appear to be very intimidating. At the time, TWA had a policy that if the glide-slope instrument failed during an ILS approach, it was acceptable to continue the approach to glide-slope inoperative limits. Without the glide-slope, the approach had to be terminated after a published time limit instead of an altitude limit. So we were making an ILS approach in instrument weather conditions to runway 14L at ORD when the glide-slope failed. The aircraft ahead of me made a missed approach. I instructed the first officer to change to the glide-slope out minimums and that I had started the clock and announced when the time to the missed approach would expire. We landed safely and taxied to the gate. This is when the fun began. The 1011 has a large cockpit and when I got out of my seat, I was about to turn and get my flight kit, but there was this large man standing right in front of me and I could not turn. Uh-oh, what did I do? The FAA inspector bent down and gave me a big hug. He told me he was impressed that I was prepared for a glide-slope failure and did not have to execute a missed approach like the aircraft ahead of us. He told me I saved a lot of money for the company and that he was going to relay the information to the chief pilot. I was dumbfounded but very thankful that I knew the policy and procedure.

THE AIR LINE PILOTS ASSOCIATION

ALPA's founders chose "Schedule with Safety" as their motto, and that theme remains central to the union's work today. TWA's MEC (Master Executive Council) Safety Committee included an Accident Investigation Committee and a Training Committee. In 1986 I was appointed as chairman of the MEC Training Committee and I reported to the MEC chairman of the Safety Committee.

Captain Bob Pastore joined me as Vice-chairman. We both owned outside training business and I felt we would represent TWA pilots well in our dealings with TWA management. Captain Pastore and I developed an excellent rapport with the

68

training center. Due to the ALPA hierarchy, I had to get permission from the Safety Chairman to have meetings with senior management pilots.

Captain Pastore and I felt strongly that the Training Committee should be independent from the Safety Committee. Our reasoning was that each and every TWA pilot was subjected to training and checking every year sometimes twice annually, and hopefully, not every pilot will have a safety issue annually. The TWA Master Executive Council agreed and made the Training Committee an independent committee responsible to the MEC. Bob and I not only felt that we were responsible for training, we were also responsible for flight standards. We train to standards. Standardization is what leads to safety. So the MEC Training and Standards Committee was created as a stand-alone committee with its own budget.

Captain Pastore and I worked with committee representatives from each of the domiciles. Bob was a great organizer and laid out the responsibilities of the committee. My initial interest was a little different. I took a special interest in pilots that found themselves in jeopardy of not completing training. We had over 4,000 pilots flying the DC-9, 727, 767, 757, L-1011, and the 747. We had instructors at the training center that gave proficiency checks and recurrent training on the different types of aircraft. We also had line check airmen that gave training and line checks on all the different types that were carrying passengers. We needed to have everyone on the same page.

In my opinion at that time, it was apparent that TWA was standardized by tradition. We had been flying airplanes safely for many years using procedures handed down from earlier generations. However, much of what we did was technique and not published procedure. Pilots could get in jeopardy because some check pilots and instructors had their own way of doing things that was not spelled out in any manuals. It was imperative that we had to standardize all the fleets. The L-1011 manual was written as though the captain flew every leg. It was important to differentiate between the pilot-flying and the pilot-not flying. If flight crew members flew by the book, they should not fail check rides. However, that meant the instructors and check airmen also had to go by the book.

The company would notify us when a crewmember was in jeopardy of not completing training. That would trigger an interview with the crewmember. So Bob and I would hopefully hear both sides of the story. In many cases, we would side with the check airman and point out to the crewmember our reasoning. Most cases were resolved but when it became chronic, we would request that the crewmember take a physical exam. Several crewmembers were retired medically before they failed to complete training. There was close cooperation between management and the MEC Training and Standards Committee.

A training failure grievance filed by a crewmember is very costly to the company and ALPA. TWA changed the captain upgrade program from the up or out policy to be able to revert back to the flight engineer position if unable to upgrade. There was a captain failure training grievance in progress when I was appointed MEC training chairman. The student captain failed to upgrade to captain on the L-1011. Although I would not have encouraged upgrading on the wide-body L-1011, I agreed to appear at the hearing on behalf of the student captain. The student captain was handled by some very tough check airmen that maybe felt he should not be upgrading on the L-1011. My defense was to blame the flight manager for the attitude and conduct of the line check airmen that he had assigned. The flight manager was in attendance at the hearing and he did not appreciate my comments in front of the big wigs at the hearing. The student captain's failure was upheld but that was not going to be the last time that I ran into that flight manager.

The MEC Training and Standards Committee met regularly with the company and we demonstrated that a positive relation with the company was good for the company and the pilots. TWA and ALPA agreed to form the TWA Pilot Training Board made up of five members. The board consisted of the chief pilots from STL and JFK, the TWA vice-president of Training, Captain Pastore and myself. The domicile chief pilots and the VP of training changed periodically, but Bob and I served until I retired in 1998 when he took my place as Chairman. Truthfully, we really accomplished many positive results. It wasn't always a pleasant job. Some crewmembers could not complete training and were advised to retire. Some instructors lost their focus and patience. There was a day we told an L-1011 instructor pilot that he was losing his instructor status and he was going back to the line. He had tears in his eyes as he said the line pilots hated him. The Pilot Training Board instituted a policy where the training center instructors had to fly the line several months every year.

It is not my position that some check airmen can be unfair. However, it can't be helped when there are personality conflicts that can result in bias. I interviewed many crewmembers that had failed to upgrade to captain or first officer. They were restricted to the flight engineer position. This was not the end of the world but not their career goals. A year or so before I retired, Captain Pastore and I worked out a one time deal with the Vice-President of Flight Operations where everyone that failed to upgrade would be given another chance. This was a very generous offer from the company to maybe rectify some unfair failures. It was predicted that many would fail again. Some failed but many succeeded and finished their career as a captain or first officer. Bob and I were very proud of ALPA's participation in this memorable show of cooperation with TWA management.

70

CHAPTER 7

B-747

TWA introduced the Boeing 747 in 1970. In 1971, I transferred from Chicago to New York so that I could fly the 747 as a first officer. First officers on the TWA 747 had to have a FAA Airline Transport Pilot Type Rating on the 747. I wanted to have that rating and get international flying experience at the same time. After a year of delightful flying the 747, I transferred back to Chicago to continue flying captain on the 880.

So about the time I was flying captain on the 767 and the L-1011, my seniority allowed me to fly on the B-747 as a captain. It was an easy check out since I already had the 747 type rating and a year flying the aircraft on international routes.

By the end of the 1980s, I was flying the 747 regularly. For awhile I maintained dual qualification with the L-1011. This meant I could fly one leg on the 747 and the next on the L1011 if the operation called for it. This could happen when the company substituted equipment. It was crazy and I ultimately let my L-1011 qualifications expire.

Captains were required to take an annual line check conducted by a TWA line check airman. It was usually put in your schedule and you were notified ahead of time as a courtesy. Well one day I showed up to fly a 747 trip from JFK to CDG in Paris. The flight manager I criticized at the training grievance showed up and told me he was giving me an unannounced check ride to Paris and back. I told him that he would not be allowed in my cockpit. The FAA has a rule that the captain can restrict anyone from the cockpit in the interest of safety. This guy was out to get me. He had a bad reputation and his nickname was "the wrong stuff." The flight manager and I walked down to the office of the chief pilot, Captain Hugh Schoelzel, who happened to be on the Pilot Training Board with me. There I explained why I would not take a check ride from this flight manager. The chief pilot said he didn't blame me, he would do the same. So I had an enjoyable flight to Paris without the flight manager aboard.

OPERATION DESERT SHIELD AND DESERT STORM

Shortly after Saddam Hussein led a well-equipped Iraqi army into Kuwait on August 2, 1990, I was in command of TWA 884 that had just landed in Tel Aviv, Israel. The crew was scheduled for a long layover but we were advised stay close to the hotel. No long sight-seeing layover, TWA wanted us to fly the airplane back to New York the next day.

Due to the large amount of military air traffic, we could not get oceanic clearance out of Tel Aviv but we took off to try get as far west as we could. Nearing Spain, we determined that we did not have enough fuel to cross the ocean. We landed for fuel in Shannon, Ireland and finally made it back to JFK. Little did I know that I would soon be involved in the operation to fly troops and equipment into Saudi Arabia in support of Operation Desert Shield.

On August 7, 1990, President George Bush ordered the organization of Operation Desert Shield in response to Iraq's invasion of Kuwait. The operation authorized a dramatic increase in U.S. troops and resources in the Persian Gulf. In 1951 President Truman issued an executive order that led to the creation of the Civil Reserve Air Fleet (CRAF). The order tasked the Department of Commerce in conjunction with the Department of Defense to formulate a plan to provide contingency airlift capabilities for the nation. The Military Airlift Command (MAC) activated the Civil Reserve Air Fleet (CRAF) for the first time to support the nation's most massive transport operation ever. This action gave MAC access to 17 commercial international long-range jets and 21 long-range cargo transports. TWA was part of the operation that provided crews and 747 airplanes. There were 14 TWA captain volunteers for CRAF, and I was one of them. When MAC activated the CRAF it assumed mission control of the flight while the airlines retained all operational control of their aircraft and crews.

Saddam was threatening the "mother of all wars" and the security for the crewmembers was unbelievable. Our identities were kept secret for the security of our families. My wife could not be told where I was going. There were many missions I flew carrying troops and live rockets. Until the end of the war, our airplanes were painted white to avoid identity with TWA. At first, I was excited to be part of the mission, but closer to the beginning of the hostilities, I became uneasy because we were transporting doctors and nurses for the expected casualties. The airlift was very successful. More than 60 percent of the troops and 25 percent of the cargo airlifted into or out of the theater was from the CRAF.

Coalition forces conducted ground combat operations in Iraq engaging with the enemy on February 17, 1991. On 27 February, Saddam ordered a retreat from Kuwait, and President Bush declared it liberated. However, an Iraqi unit at Kuwait International Airport appeared not to have received the message and fiercely resisted. US Marines had to fight for hours before securing the airport, after which Kuwait was declared secure.

We soon prepared to fly the troops home. It was my honor and pleasure to carry members of the 1st Marine Division that participated in the combat at Kuwait International Airport. Their unit had suffered casualties.

We landed at Norton Air Force Base in California.

We finally landed in Honolulu, Hawaii.

Flying American troops during Operation Desert Shield and Desert Storm was an unforgettable experience. Although it may have been against company regulations, I always allowed visitors to the cockpit during cruise flight. Thank God it was a short war.

TWA FLIGHT 800

TWA flight 800 crashed into the Atlantic Ocean on July 17, 1996. During a layover in London that same night while waiting to fly back to St. Louis, I was awakened in the middle of the night. TWA operations told me that one of my flight attendant's husband was on flight 800 and TWA wanted her to fly to New York instead of St. Louis. I turned on the television, saw the carnage, and realized this was a real disaster for TWA. As Training and Standards chairman, I was invited to participate in the accident investigation. I declined. Now I wish that I had not declined. There are many TWA crewmembers that do not believe the results of the FBI and the NTSB investigation.

LIVING THE DREAM

Good judgements come from experience, and a lot of that experience comes from bad judgements. Next to the B-747, I flew captain on the B-727 more than any other TWA airplane. Once flying into Albuquerque, New Mexico on a B-727, my first officer was new and fairly in-experienced. He was making a visual approach and I realized he was too high. So I took the airplane controls and aggressively put the airplane back into the so called landing slot. Then I gave the controls back to the first officer so he could continue the approach and landing. Bad call on my part. He made a bad approach and landing because he had mentally stopped flying as soon as I took the controls. It only happened one more time in my career with the first officer getting too close to mountains flying into Palm Springs, California. Once I took over, I never gave the controls back

Over the years of flying, I found that probably the hardest and most stressful part of being a captain occurs while on the ground. First off, landing on an icy runway gets your attention. But it is worse to taxi on an icy taxiway because you have to turn the airplane and maybe it does not want to turn. Several of my gray hairs come from a very narrow and elevated taxiway in Pittsburgh. If you slide off that taxiway, you are going down a deep ravine.

Do I really want to relate this experience? Hubris is defined as exaggerated self-confidence. OK, it was the last leg of a three day B-727 trip that terminated at Chicago O'Hare. We were all anxious to get home. To get home, we had to get to our automobiles that were parked at the TWA hangar on the far side of the airport. Crew busses ran every 20 minutes between the hanger and the terminal on a set schedule. The crew bus driver left on schedule even if you were running to catch the bus.

So we landed and taxied off the runway to make a circle around the terminals toward the TWA gates. A very light rain had just started. OK, if I hustle we can make the next crew bus. As I rounded the curve by the United terminal at a good clip, there was an executive jet that had stopped on the taxiway because he was lost. You don't expect this on a busy taxiway. Hit the brakes and start sliding. We stopped but I had several more gray hairs. Just to save 20 minutes. Duh! You do not stop flying the airplane until you are parked at the gate and the engines are shut down. That is a lesson that I would like to pass on.

IT'S AWESOME

What was it like to be an airline pilot for TWA? My answer would be "It's awesome." Maybe not so awesome for my wife, Sue. She raised our two beautiful daughters basically on her own. Sure, when I was home, I might be home for several days. When I was gone, Sue had to deal with flooded basements, broken refrigerators, dead batteries, and many more calamities all alone.

For most of my more that 34 year career, TWA treated their pilots very well. Howard Hughes owned TWA when I was hired in 1964. Since he was an accomplished pilot, it is my belief that he admired pilots. We were considered a 'captain's 'airline meaning the TWA captain had command of the operation of the flight. TWA flew around the world, and whether in Africa, Asia, Europe, or the U.S., the captain was in charge. If pilots for the large domestic airlines needed assistance, it was just a phone call away. Not so easy if you are in Bombay or Hong Kong. At TWA, the captain was in charge of the entire operation. TWA had a VIP lounge at many airports called the Ambassador Club. TWA captains were members of the club. Most airlines would not think of letting pilots into the company's VIP lounges.

TWA
Ambassadors Club
1032 983 92 003
CAPT. JEROME LAWLER
MEMBER SINCE 11/92 VALID THROUGH 1/99

The 747 was-and is-probably the most easily recognizable jet airliner. The pilot's contract with TWA limited our flying time to 75 flight hours a month. Four trips from New York to Paris a month was close to 75 hours. Each trip took 3 days with about about a 28 hour layover in Paris. My trip of choice was from St. Louis to London and back to St.Louis after a 28 hour layover.

Flying the "queen of the skies" was an incredible experience. The airplane is enormous. We carried 2 pilots and a flight engineer along with up to 20 flight attendants. There were over 430 passenger seats. Since the weight of the airplane is so important, we measured the fuel in thousands of pounds. The TWA 747 could carry 342,000 pounds of fuel. That is 51,000 gallons. Whew! The aircraft could weigh 75,000 pounds at takeoff.

Before we fly, we have to taxi to the runway. The cockpit sits three stories high which is great for visibility. The B-727 has 4 wheels on it's main landing gear. The B-747 has 16 main landing gear wheels. To aid in steering on the ground, 8 of those wheels turn in the opposite direction of the nose wheel steering. The Inertial Navigation Systems indicates the groundspeed during taxi. Sitting so high in the cockpit, it is very easy to taxi much faster than than your senses tell you. It is very important to limit the ground speed to 25 mph especially during turns to avoid damage to the wheels.

Another thing to think about sitting so high in the cockpit. How do we evacuate? The captain may not always be the first to know the need for an emergency evacuation. If the nature of the emergency requires immediate action, the crew member will initiate the evacuation alarm system. If the airplane is moving on the ground, the captain will stop the airplane and shut down the engines. The general evacuation plan consists of the flight attendants operating their respective doors and slides, while the cockpit crew is deployed throughout the cabin to command and direct the evacuation. To get to the main cabin, the cockpit crew has to race down the circular staircase. The FAA requires a full-scale emergency evacuation demonstration that simulates an aborted takeoff. TWA must show that the aircraft emergency equipment, and emergency procedures allow the evacuation of the aircraft at full seating capacity, including crewmembers, in 90 seconds or less. With 400 passengers, that can be a challenge.

According to Boeing statistical studies, 16% of fatal accidents occur during takeoff and initial climb, while 29% occur during the approach and landing. In my mind, the landing is more fun to fly, but the takeoff is more critical than the landing. That is because on takeoff we have to take a very heavy aircraft loaded with fuel from a standing start and get to a decision speed where we either abort the takeoff or continue the takeoff. An engine failure on takeoff is more dangerous because the aircraft may not yet be flying. During landing, the aircraft is already at flying speed if there is an engine failure or a need to abort the landing.

So what is it like to handle the takeoff in an airplane that weighs 775,000 pounds with over 400 passengers? It is "awesome." First off, you prepare mentally and have confidence that you can handle any emergency during takeoff. Before takeoff, I brief the cockpit crew on an aborted takeoff or initial actions if there is an engine failure or engine fire after V1.

Even if the first officer is handling the flight controls and is responsible for flying the aircraft, TWA policy mandates that the captain handles the throttles during the takeoff. It is the captain's decision to abort or continue the takeoff. OK, it is my leg and we are cleared onto the runway. Look down the runway. "Cleared for Takeoff." Be mentally prepared to react to an emergency, like an engine failure or an engine fire during takeoff. Release the brakes. My right hand grabs the four throttles and pushes them forward. It takes a bit to get started. The B-727 engine produced about 16,000 pounds of thrust. Each of these 747 engines produce about 46,000 pounds of thrust.

There are four engine instruments that we monitor during the takeoff. The top instrument indicates the Engine Pressure Ratio gauge or EPR. It measures the ratio of how much air pressure enters the front of the engine compared to how much air pressure exits the engine providing the thrust. There are movable markings on the EPR gauges for indicating a set target thrust. The instrument below indicates the temperature of the exhaust gas temperature or EGT. This is the temperature of the gas exiting the engine. The EGT is limited during takeoff to 915^0 Centigrade because that is the heat on the turbine blades. Excess heat can damage the blades.

So I push the throttles up toward the markings set on the EPR gauges used for takeoff thrust. We need the engines all operating at the same thrust for directional control, so I command the flight engineer to trim the throttles. He can control the throttles from below my hand. He reaches below my arm and hand to trim the throttles. This is an exciting time for me and it can give me goose bumps on my arm. I hope the flight

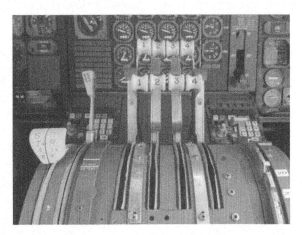

engineer does not see them. I still get goose bumps just talking about it. It is not exciting like a roller-coaster ride. It is exciting because there is a tremendous amount of physical forces in action that require concentration and situational awareness. Think about the aircraft tires. Airplane takeoff speeds are designed to ensure the liftoff speed does not exceed the tire speed rating. Most 747 tires are rated at 235 miles per hour. We use knots on our speed indicator so the maximum ground speed at liftoff is 204 knots.

Going from 0 knots to 204 knots weighing over 700,000 pounds takes time and lots of runway. In our TWA training, if there is an emergency, we are taught to react immediately. Don't sit there and say why is this happening. Taking off a heavy 747 with hundreds of passengers and thousands of gallons of fuel is a big deal. With my right hand pushing the 4 throttles forward, my left hand is on the tiller that controls the nose wheel steering to keep the airplane on the centerline of the runway. As we accelerate, the first officer calls out "80 knots" when we reach that speed. With the increased airflow over the rudder, I can take my hand off the tiller and use the rudder pedals to control the nose wheel steering.

With my left hand on the control wheel, I may lower a wing into a strong crosswind. Next comes the first officer's call of "V1." Now we are committed to fly and I can take my right hand off the throttles and put it on the control yoke. Continuing to accelerate, the next call from the first officer is "Vr." This is rotation speed at which I pull back on the control column to lift the nose off the runway at 3^0 per second to a target of 15^0 nose up on the attitude indicator displayed on the screens in front of each pilot. The nose wheel lifts off but the other 16 tires are still accelerating on the ground. This rotation is not an abrupt maneuver. If you rotate too fast, you can scrape the tail on the ground. If you rotate to slow you can exceed the tire speed limit. It takes about 4 more seconds for the 16 main gear wheels to lift off the ground. The next speed we are looking for is V2. This is known as takeoff safety speed because the airplane will still climb in the event of an engine failure. When the rate of climb indicator shows we are climbing and the airspeed indicates V2, I command "Gear up." Now we climb at V2 + 10 knots to 1000 feet above the field elevation.

OK, we are safely in the air and flying. I don't know about you, but that was exciting for me. At 1000 feet, I lower the nose to accelerate and retract the flaps and climb to 3000 feet at V2 +100 knots. The flight engineer sets climb thrust and we continue to climb using climb speed. OK, we just AVIATED. Now we must NAVIGATE. Most airports have complicated departures for noise abatement that requires immediate attention. In the meantime we COMMUNICATE with departure control and continue on the flight to our destination.

It is easy to put the airplane on the autopilot. My preference is to hand fly the 747 to cruising altitude which can take up to 30 minutes. Since I cannot maintain cruising altitude as well as the autopilot, I engage the autopilot when we reach cruising altitude.

THE FUN PART AND MOST CHALLENGING

That would be the approach and landing a jet airliner. Jets were relatively new in the 1960s and I watched a year of 707 landings from the flight engineer seat. It seemed to me that there was a lot of flight control and throttle movement in the early days of jet operations. Flying a small airplane like that would make you sick. When it was my turn to go to first officer training, my instructor told me to learn by watching the autopilot fly an approach in the simulator. Of course there was little wind, but the controls and throttles hardly moved during the final approach on the autopilot before landing.

These are big airplanes so, you would think they must be a lot of work to fly. Watching the autopilot fly an approach doesn't look like it is working hard at all. Let's try it that way. As little movement of the controls as possible. Pressure, not movement of the controls.

The maximum landing weight of the TWA 747 is 564,000 pounds. Based on the landing weight, we have a landing reference speed. We call this Bug speed which is put on each pilot's airspeed indicator. Generally jet airliners are in the landing configuration with wheels down and landing flaps at 5 miles from the runway and at 1500 feet. If the airplane is in trim, meaning nothing changes if you take your hands off the controls, you are on a good approach toward a good landing. The pilot needs to control three things from now to landing. Speed is incredibly important. We want our airspeed to be Bug + 5 knots. We also have to be lined up with the centerline of the runway. So we have to look out the window to see how we are doing. The window becomes another instrument at this point. So if we keep the wings level, we should stay lined up with the runway.

Remember our attitude indicator. It is still the main instrument in the scan. Each jet type is different but we fly the approach with a nose up attitude that keeps the airspeed at Bug + 5 if we do not change the thrust with the throttles. The trick to make it look easy is staying in trim. This requires some effort. For example, if we lower the nose, the airspeed will increase. That will require a change in thrust to keep the speed at Bug + 5. That is going to change the trim on the airplane tail. Now we start chasing things. we raise the nose, start to slow up now we need more thrust. A little crosswind and we are drifting off the centerline so we lower a wing. Ok, now what. Back to the attitude indicator to check the wings and nose up indicator. Check the airspeed indicator. Check the rate of descent indicator. It should show a descent rate of around 700 feet per minute. You don't need to look at the compass now because you are using the front window for direction. Here is where a smooth pilot demonstrates finesse by making pressures on the controls and throttles instead of big movements.

At some point, we are cleared to land. Over the runway, we are no longer looking at the aiming point. We are looking at the far end of the runway to judge our closure rate with the runway. The landing flare maneuver is initiated at about 30 feet above

the runway to reduce the runway closure rate while reducing or closing the throttles as you touchdown. The nose up pitch attitude at touchdown is approximately to 6 degrees. This is not the time to be making large control movements. The landing gear is tilted so that the rear wheels touchdown first and can soften the landing.

Since the wings are still developing lift at touchdown, we use spoilers on the wings that extend vertically upwards to destroy the lift on the wings. The spoilers also put the weight of the aircraft on the wheels so that the brakes may be employed. Immediately after the main gear touches down, observe auto-spoiler operation and simultaneously raise all reverse levers applying maximum reverse thrust as the nose wheel is being lowered to the runway. The pilot not flying calls out at "80 knots" during the landing roll. At 80 knots, start reducing reverse thrust smoothly to reach reverse idle by 60 knots. Be out of reverse thrust at completion of landing roll and prior to runway turn off. By now I am familiar with all the taxi routes and proceed to the passenger gate while doing the After Landing Checklist. At the gate we shut down the engines and do the Secure Cockpit Checklist. Wow!

Six months before my scheduled retirement in September 1998, TWA retired the majestic Boeing 747. So it was back to the B-767. Since I had not flown the 767 for more than 7 years, I was required to go through the entire training curriculum of

ground school, simulator, and aircraft transition. Since I last flew the 767, w
acquired the B-757 and I would need training on it. Captain Hobie Tomlinson, the 74
fleet manager, was not 767 qualified and he asked me to be his simulator partner i
training. Since I already had the 767 type rating, all I really needed was a proficienc
check but I agreed to fly several training periods for Hobie's benefit. After simulato
training, Captain John Zaeske was waiting to complete my line qualification. We fle\
from St. Louis to California and back on the 757. The next day we flew to Paris an
back on the 767 and I was fully qualified.

My wife, Sue, accompanied me on my retirement flight from St. Louis to London and back. The STL Chief Pilot and the VP of training escorted my wife onto the flight. In London, the station manager escorted my wife through customs and onto the waiting crew bus. It was delightful last flight.

To go from Pre-med to B-747 captain, a lot of things had to go right. First off, in 1964, age between 20 and 30 years with good eye-sight. TWA required 20-20 vision. Also you needed excellent health. With a physical every ‹ months, TWA did not want to lose you for medical reasons. Next you needed a clea‹ law-enforcement record. No drugs or alcohol problems. No disciplinary problems i‹ school. A good attitude really helps. There has to be a willingness to learn and accep‹ the airline's policy and procedures. A good reputation makes life easier. When yo‹ work for a good reputation, your good reputation works for you.

After 34 years with TWA, my going from a single engine civilian pilot to fly captai‹ on 7 different TWA jet airliners is a tribute to the outstanding training TWA wa‹ famous for. I am proud of the relationship built between TWA management pilots an‹ the representatives of the Air Line Pilots Association. We worked well together fo‹ the good of the flight crews. It was an honor and a privilege to be a TWA pilot.

TRANS WORLD AIRLINES ◆ FLIGHT OPERATIONS

TWA TWA TWA TWA TWA TWA

In appreciation of
Loyal and Dedicated Service Honors

Captain

𝕵𝖊𝖗𝖔𝖒𝖊 𝕮. 𝕷𝖆𝖜𝖑𝖊𝖗

Who Has Served with Distinction from
June 15, 1964
To
September 12, 1998

TWA TWA TWA TWA TWA TWA

Chief Pilot

Vice President Flight Operations

2

About the Author

Jerry Lawler earned his Private Pilot license in 1959 while enrolled in college. He joined TWA in 1964 as a Lockheed Constellation flight engineer, progressed to Convair 880 first officer, and upgraded to Convair 880 captain in 1968. For the next 30 years he flew captain on the B-707, B-727, B-757, B-767, B-747 and Lockheed L-1011 on both domestic and international routes. Although a loyal TWA employee, Jerry was active in the Air Line Pilots Association, serving as a member of the ALPA Board of Directors and Chairman of the Training and Standards Committee. In 1998, The Trans World Airlines AWARD OF EXCELLENCE was presented to Jerry in recognition of outstanding performance in the Captain position.

In 1985, Jerry became an FAA Designated Written Test Examiner. He started an aviation school that prepared applicants to take the FAA written test required to become a flight engineer and the written test required to become a captain. The school, Avtest, successfully trained thousands of pilot applicants to pass the required exams. Jerry authored two training manuals, the FLIGHT ENGINEER Programmed Learning Guide and the AIRLINE TRANSPORT PILOT Programmed Learning Guide. The school closed in 2013 when the FAA changed the requirements to take the exams.

In 2010, the FAA honored Jerry with The Wright Brothers "Master Pilot" Award for practicing and promoting safe aircraft operations for 50 consecutive years.

Made in the USA
Monee, IL
03 August 2020